A VETERAN SAVING THE TEENS OF PUNJAB

Col (Dr.) Rajinder Singh

Aditi Rana

ISBN
Paperback 979-8-89610-999-0
Hardcase 979-8-89777-852-2

*91-year-old veteran saving the teens of
Punjab from drugs*

Dr. (Col.) Rajinder Singh's journey serves as
a profound reminder to humanity that compassion
is the ultimate path forward.

Contents

Foreword

Drug addiction is not just a personal struggle; it is a societal crisis that demands urgent and compassionate intervention. In Northern India, where addiction has devastated countless lives, one man has stood as a light of hope—Dr. (Col.) Rajinder Singh. His journey is not just that of a psychiatrist but of a visionary, a healer, and a relentless warrior against one of the most pressing issues of our time.

For over five decades, Dr. Singh has dedicated his life to the service of others, offering not just medical treatment but a holistic path to recovery—one that nurtures the mind, body, and soul. His work transcends conventional psychiatric care, weaving together medical expertise with spiritual healing, ensuring that every individual battling addiction is met with dignity, understanding, and support.

Through this book, readers will witness the extraordinary resilience of a man who has touched over 35,000 lives, giving them a second chance at a future free from the chains of addiction. His relentless commitment to combating substance abuse, his pioneering efforts in mental health care, and his selfless service through charitable initiatives serve as a testament to what one individual can achieve with conviction and compassion.

This narrative is more than just an account of addiction treatment—it is an inspiring chronicle of transformation, a call to action for society to recognize and address this deep-seated issue with empathy and urgency. The stories within these pages shed light on the power of hope and the impact of one man's tireless mission to heal, restore, and uplift those in need.

As you turn these pages, may you be inspired by Dr. Rajinder Singh's determination, his boundless compassion, and his indomitable spirit. May this book ignite a sense of responsibility within each of us to contribute, in whatever way we can, to the fight against addiction and the pursuit of a healthier, more hopeful tomorrow.

Preface

Indomitable Spirit

In the quiet corners of Chandigarh, enveloped by the serenity of Gurdwara Guru Tegh Bahadur in Sector 34, resides a venerable soul whose life's narrative reads like a symphony of healing and hope. Dr. Rajinder Singh, at the age of 90, stands as a living testament to the power of compassion, the essence of the human spirit, and the steadfast promise to a cause larger than oneself.

> *'Life is a journey, and the noblest destination is the service of others.'*
>
> *- Dr. Rajinder Singh*

The pages of this biography unfold not just the chronicles of a distinguished psychiatrist and social worker, but also the epic saga of a man who, for over five decades, has sculpted the contours of mental health and drug de-addiction in India. His spiritual and humane touch has been a balm for as many as 50,000 souls.

In the quietude of his charitable dispensary, nestled within the pious walls of Gurdwara Guru Tegh Bahadur, Dr. Rajinder Singh has not only dispensed medical care but also woven a world of hope, love, and support for those navigating the tumultuous terrain of recovery. His practice, rooted in compassion, transcends the clinical boundaries, embracing the spiritual essence of healing.

> ***'In the silence between heartbeats lies the space where healing begins.'***
>
> *- Dr. Rajinder Singh*

Having retired from the Indian Army in 1991, Dr. Rajinder Singh seamlessly transitioned from the disciplined cadence of military life to the role of a voluntary director of two drug de-addiction centers, a mantle he has worn with grace since 2004. It is here that his legacy of combating substance abuse flourishes, offering a lifeline to both men and women ensnared by the clutches of addiction.

> ***'The true measure of a society is found in how it treats its most vulnerable members.'***
>
> *- Dr. Rajinder Singh*

The corridors of his mind are a repository of wisdom cultivated during his tenure in the Indian Army. Dr. Rajinder Singh served with a spirit of camaraderie and duty, a spirit that continues to permeate his persona, while empathetic understanding and spiritual guidance form the bedrock of the holistic care he provides.

Beyond the confines of his professional practice, he has etched his impact on the literary canvas too. Two books, penned with the ink of experience and empathy, stand as a guiding light, illuminating the path to understanding and overcoming drug addiction. His motivational campaigns, a clarion call against the perils of substance abuse, not only earned him global acclaim but also became evidence of the efficacy of his efforts.

In the hallowed halls of recognition, Dr Rajinder Singh stands adorned with a Lifetime Achievement Award, a laurel bestowed upon a life dedicated to the well-being of individuals and communities. It is an echo of countless lives transformed under his benevolent gaze.

'The greatest reward in life is knowing that one has made a difference.'

- Dr. Rajinder Singh

The labyrinth of his experiences, anecdotes, and triumphs transcends the ordinary; Dr. (Col.) Rajinder Singh is indeed a legend. This is not just a narrative; it is an odyssey of compassion, a saga of change, and above all, a fine example of the indomitable spirit of a man who has lived a life larger than life itself.

Chapter 1

Roots of Innocence

Dr. Rajinder Singh's life, from his humble beginnings in Lahore, Pakistan, is an example of the enduring bonds of family and the transformative power of education. Part of a joint family, his childhood was marked by the warmth of kinship and the guidance of his elder brother—a figure of wisdom, a guru, and a mentor.

Dr. Rajinder Singh was born in 1934 in the village of Daburji, located in the Batala tehsil near Dera Baba Nanak in Punjab's Gurdaspur district. His father, S. Bhagat Singh 'Matwala', and mother, Sardarni Kartar Kaur, hailed from a modest, devout Sikh family with an agricultural background.

Recalling his early days, Dr. Singh fondly remembers the simple yet thorough moments of walking to Dedhgawar Primary School. At the tender age of seven years, he traversed this daily journey on foot, a testament to the strength of a joint household with five brothers.

In the corridors of the Sikh National College, where Dr. Rajinder Singh's elder brother embarked on their educational maneuver in Lahore, memories abound of sitting on *chatai,* absorbing the teachings in Urdu. Despite the modest surroundings, the bond between siblings served as a source of strength and camaraderie, surpassing the challenges of their upbringing.

Their home was a simple mud house shared with extended family, one that echoed with the laughter of children and the warmth of shared dreams. Amidst the humble family backgrounds, financial constraints, and nature of their existence, dictated by their father's postings in the railways, the family found peace and happiness in togetherness as well as the steady support of Dr. Rajinder Singh's elder brother. It was this reinforcement that paved the way for his education, as his elder brother assumed the role of a father figure.

Dr. Rajinder Singh fondly talks about his brothers; his younger brother, Surinder Singh, known affectionately as 'Mema', was blessed with strikingly good looks and a fair complexion, earning him the playful nickname suggestive of being born to a 'mem' (a figurative term for a White English lady).

Despite his charm, Mema frequently faced physical reprimands from his elder brother, Gurbaksh Singh, due to his tendency to neglect his studies. However, Dr. Rajinder Singh's achievement of becoming a doctor upon completing his MBBS inspired Mema to take his education more seriously. Determined not to fall behind, he diligently pursued studies and eventually completed a bachelor's degree in engineering and later earned acclaim as an accomplished electrical engineer.

S. Bhagat Singh (1898-1977), Rajinder Singh's father, hailed from the village of Daburji in Punjab's Gurdaspur district, where he grew into a handsome young man. In the absence of a school in his native village, he pursued his education at a school in Dehargawar, a neighboring village. Notably robust, he caught the eye of British recruitment teams who sought physically strong individuals for labor-intensive roles. At the age of around 17-18 years, he secured a position as a laborer at the Railway Loco Shed in Lahore, chosen for his physical prowess.

An exemplar of contentment and benevolence, S. Bhagat Singh was deeply committed to social causes, aiding the less fortunate. On one occasion, he provided refuge to a widowed woman left destitute after her husband perished in a rail accident, showcasing rare compassion and empathy.

S. Bhagat Singh never resorted to physical discipline with his children, even in challenging circumstances. Known for his devoutness, he often recited self-composed poems that honored the valor and sacrifices of Sikh Gurus and warriors in the face of Mughal tyranny as well as invasions. He fervently encouraged youth to embrace Sikh principles, imparting the timeless wisdom of the great Sikh Gurus.

S. Bhagat Singh 'Matwala', characterized by his sober and composed demeanor, possessed a captivating charm and imposing presence during his youthful days. Despite having received education only up to the primary level, his dedication, moderation, and self-discipline paved the way for a successful career in the Indian Railways. His noble philanthropic endeavors and spiritual inclinations endeared him to both colleagues and superiors wherever he served, earning him regular commendations and promotions until his retirement from a respectable position.

Beyond his professional achievements, S. Bhagat Singh was a multifaceted individual, known for his prowess as a poet and writer. He exemplified values of love, truthfulness, and tolerance in his everyday life. The family's esteemed lineage was further stamped by the historical honor bestowed upon their ancestor, Sardar Sukha

Singh, of village Balakeechak, who was recognized by Maharaja Ranjit Singh with a grant of 64 acres of land for his valor, following the victory over Multan in 1818.

Sardarni Kartar Kaur, S. Bhagat Singh's life partner, embodied simplicity and kindness, sacrificing everything for the betterment of their children's future. While kneading dough for rotis (chapatis), she would always recite "Waheguru Waheguru", infusing the food with a divine essence that blessed her five children like Amrit (nectar). She strongly believed in the impact of food on one's thoughts, mind, and actions. The adage *Jaisa Ann Vaisa Mann* (जैसा अन्न वैसा मन) aptly captures this belief, as the nourishment food provides also carries the wishes, longings, and inner perceptions of the one who prepares it.

Her relentless efforts bore fruit as all five of their sons received a comprehensive education. Dr. Rajinder Singh, the second eldest among them, is accompanied by his brothers: S. Gurbaksh Singh, M.A. L.L.B, the eldest; S. Surinder Singh, Deputy General Manager, M.I.E.; S. Mahinder Pal Singh, artist, A.I.R.; and S. Paramjit Singh, M.Sc. (Geology), Director, Geological Survey of India.

S. Bhagat Singh's poetic endeavors were fueled by the momentous life of Guru Gobind Singh Ji, whose unparalleled legacy served as a wellspring of inspiration. Additionally, he drew motivation from the Gurdwara Reforms Movement, which unfolded from 1920 to 1925, further igniting his passion for composing poems centered on themes of religion and valor.

The Gurdwara Reforms Movement of the early 1920s was a fervent religious crusade aimed at liberating Sikh religious shrines from the control of *mahants* or priests.

The culmination of this movement came with the passage of the Gurdwara Act in 1925, which entrusted the Shiromani Gurdwara Parbandhak Committee (SGPC), a representative body of Sikhs, with the custodianship of significant and historical Sikh religious sites.

S. Bhagat Singh's pride in his Sikh identity was profound. The corrupt practices of gurdwara *mahants* deeply wounded the Sikh community, prompting him to channel his anguish into poetic expression. He witnessed the sacrifices of countless Sikhs during the nonviolent Gurdwara Reforms Movement, which left an indelible mark on his heart. Despite facing intolerable atrocities, the confidence and tolerance of the Sikh community remained unshaken.

In his poetry, S. Bhagat Singh eloquently portrays the magnetic and charismatic persona of Guru Gobind Singh, emphasizing his devotion to the Almighty, fearlessness, patriotism, and willingness to bear immense hardships for the oppressed, all with a smile on his face. He holds in high esteem the bold and fearless warriors who sacrificed their lives for the nation and their faith, firmly believing in the transformative power of courage and determination.

The poet's compositions, originally in Urdu script, were meticulously compiled into Gurmukhi script by his eldest son, S. Gurbaksh Singh, showcasing the poet's intellect and ingenuity through his innovative use of language.

As Dr. Rajinder Singh reflects on his formative years, his story emerges as a testimony to the life force of the human spirit and the enduring power of family bonds. Through the trials and tribulations of their humble beginnings, the siblings found strength in each other, forging a path toward a better tomorrow and the belief that education is the key to unlocking a world of possibilities.

"I have some faded but all good memories of our days in Lahore. We had Muslim neighbors. We were living in government quarters as my father was in the railways. When I used to go to school, I was bullied for being differently dressed with my turban. But there were many great memories. We had cordial relations with our neighbors. My *bua* (paternal aunt) was also living with us, along with her two children. I also remember the railway station where my father was working. We always used to go there and have a lot of fun. And all of us used to visit our ancestral village by cycle. We had a house there. But due to my father's job, we couldn't live at that place. We kept changing our houses," Dr. Singh recollects.

After the partition, Dr. Rajinder Singh's family shifted to Ludhiana. He sadly shares about the massacre during the partition. Many people lost their lives during that colossal tragedy. Fortunately, his family came safely to Ludhiana as his father was in the railways. They hid in the coal chamber of the train, so they managed to survive. Later, his father got a job at Ludhiana Railways. He was just 13 years old at that time. The whole family stayed at the central location of the water supply in Ludhiana. The place used to cater to many habitations of railways' employees. There were no private/family bathrooms; there was only one common toilet for many people and most of the time they had to wait for their turn. There was only one source of water supply for more than 20 families living in railway quarters. The government quarter had only one room and one verandah, while the families comprised eight to nine people. There was no furniture, no attached bathroom, just one hall.

"I was admitted to Malwa Khalsa School, from where I passed the matriculation exam conducted by Punjab University."

Dr. Singh's elder brother used to teach him and take care of all his younger siblings as well as the family. "It was my elder brother who educated me. He always took extraordinary interest in all his brothers' education."

His quest into the medical field began with his admission to Government College, Ludhiana, in FSc (Faculty of Science). After successfully completing this stage, he secured admission to further his studies in Amritsar. This significant milestone occurred around 1950, a time when the admissions process was markedly different from today's competitive standards. Dr. Rajinder Singh reminisces about a simpler time when admission to Medical College Amritsar was based solely on academic performance, without the stress of intense competition. He vividly recalls the straightforward process of applying for admission by writing a postcard expressing his desire to pursue medicine, accompanied by details of his academic achievements. The response he received, confirming his acceptance, marked the beginning of his extraordinary plunge into the medical profession.

He remembers his fees were 190 rupees for a year. Dr. Singh went there and found out that he would not be able to get admission, as he was short of age by two to three months and did not meet the age criterion for the admission to medical college, Amritsar. Coming back, Dr. Rajinder joined BSC in the same college from where he did his Faculty of Science (FSc), and he got admission to the medical college the next year on the merit of the previous year. He started staying with a relative in Amritsar. His father and brother had promised his aunt that they would soon shift him to the hostel. However, they couldn't do so because of a financial crunch.

Dr. Rajinder Singh did not have many relatives in Amritsar. He stayed with the same aunt (*tai*) with whom they stayed when the whole family had moved to the place. The promises of him shifting to a hostel soon kept changing, as the family didn't have any funds to support the same.

He used to walk eight to nine kilometers to college. "She was my Tai (aunt). At first, with the unkept promises. She used to taunt me every day for not shifting to a hostel, but those were never directed toward me. It was for my father and brother. She was fond of me. And as I stayed there until the completion of my studies, the attachment grew and the taunts faded."

Dr. Rajinder graduated from college and went on to study psychiatry. He did his house job in both surgery and medicine at Rajindra Medical College & Hospital in Patiala for one year. He wanted to serve people. It was not a mainstream choice to opt for psychiatry at that time. However, during his training period, he was inclined toward it and decided to pursue psychiatry as a career.

He embarked on his service in Amritsar under the guidance of Dr. Vidyasagar, the father of Indian psychiatry and the esteemed head of the Mental Hospital in Amritsar during that era. Dr. Rajinder Singh's keenness soon caught the attention of the Punjab Civil Medical Services (PCMS), leading to his temporary relocation from the city. However, as the mental hospital faced a shortage of personnel, Dr. Vidyasagar recommended his transfer back to Amritsar.

It was during this period, in the year 1961, that he entered the sacred bond of marriage yet faced challenges as his spouse, a senior colleague from college, struggled to reconcile with his profession and transfers.

Despite his financial constraints, with a meager salary of 200 rupees and the responsibility of his younger siblings' education resting on his shoulders, he pursued his passion for psychiatry. However, the dream of further education at National Institute of Mental Health and Neurological Sciences (NIMHANS) Bangalore remained unfulfilled, despite getting admission to the college.

When the emergency was declared in 1962 during the Indo-China War, Dr. Rajinder Singh joined the Indian Army, responding to the call of the nation. Later, while staying in the army, he also fulfilled his dream of doing postgraduate studies in psychiatry, as he was posted to various field areas and was encouraged by the experience. He earned a place at AFMC (Armed Forces Medical College), where he completed the Advanced Course in Psychiatry at AFMC Pune and qualified for DPM (Diploma in Psychological Medicine) from Medical College Pune.

His career path led him to various corners of the country, from Lucknow to Chandigarh, Bareilly to Guwahati, each stint enriching his understanding of human behavior. Years later, his steadfast purpose culminated in the attainment of an MD degree from PGI, a pinnacle of achievement in his illustrious career.

As a Senior Advisor in Psychiatry, he embraced retirement, reflecting on a lifelong adventure driven by an insatiable curiosity about the intricacies of human behavior, a quest that became the cornerstone of his professional legacy.

Dr. Rajinder Singh's family dynamics were as diverse as they were inspiring. His elder brother, anchored to the simple living of village life, stood as evidence of the varied paths one could choose. While his siblings eventually found their homes in other cities, his youngest brother remained in the same city as him, living nearby.

Dr. Rajinder Singh's elder brother, a constant presence of guidance and support, fueled his aspirations, reinforcing the importance of resilience amidst life's challenges. Despite initial discontent from his kids for what they perceived as a lack of formal education, his philosophy of self-learning and embracing life's uncertainties resonated deeply.

Financial constraints initially deterred Dr. Rajinder Singh from pursuing medicine, yet his elder brother's solid encouragement manifested through poignant letters invoking the wisdom of historical figures, keeping his ambitions aflame. The tangible expressions of affection and encouragement, preserved in those cherished letters, remain a demonstration of the bond they shared. Meanwhile, his younger brother, Surender Singh, epitomized a life of evolving from a lineman in Bhakra Nangal Dam to a revered engineer propelled by newfound scholarly pursuits. Similarly, his other siblings carved their niches in diverse fields, from broadcasting to geology, each embodying the spirit of strength and grit instilled by their shared upbringing.

His mother was an absolutely simple, devoted lady. She was illiterate. At that time, paying a fee of 2.5 rupees was difficult, but she used to knit and pay it. She was very affectionate and warm.

His father S. Bhagat Singh, an ardent devotee of Guru Gobind Singh Ji, wrote poems of valor and sacrifice of the Sikh heroes.

"We have also published his book and poems. We collected those papers and translated them from Urdu to Punjabi. He has written about the sacrifices of Sikhs in his texts. We have a foundation in his name. His poems are recited by our students," shared Dr. Rajinder.

Three key figures in Dr. Rajinder Singh's family significantly shaped his life's trajectory. His mother, despite lacking formal education, epitomized selflessness and care; she always prioritized her children's well-being. Her life post-marriage was marked by discomfort due to discord with her sister-in-law, who resided in the same household. This strained relationship often subjected Dr. Rajinder Singh's mother to torment from her sister-in-law, further compounded by the latter's three children (two boys and a girl) also living under the same roof, thereby increasing the parental responsibilities. The friction between the mother-in-law and daughter-in-law only exacerbated the situation. His paternal grandmother and paternal aunt, his mother's mother-in-law and sister-in-law, had very cordial relations between them, and they virtually dominated the house. So, his mother lived in isolation for a long time.

Unfortunately, mental health challenges plagued Dr. Rajinder Singh's mother, impairing her ability to manage household responsibilities, a struggle compounded by domestic strife. She remained detached from worldly possessions, embodying qualities of character and contentment that a saintly relative once likened her to a divine soul.

Dr. Rajinder Singh's maternal uncle, Jaimal Singh, once proposed to his father the idea of entering into a second marriage with a widow residing in Kotli, his maternal grandparents' village. The intention behind this suggestion was to alleviate the cooking-related challenges arising from the interference of Dr. Rajinder Singh's paternal aunt. But his father outrightly refused to accept this suggestion, narrating a couplet:

"Whose arms you have pledged to hold in life, do not leave even if you have to lay down your head. Guru Tegh Bahadur said it is better to get buried in the earth than to forsake your Dharma."

Dr. Rajinder Singh's early years were shaped by adversity, particularly in accessing education. The absence of electricity in his family home meant that he had to study in the faint glow of an earthen lamp. His father's employment in the railways led to frequent relocations, and the family eventually settled in Lahore (now in Pakistan). There, he continued his education at SD High School from seventh to tenth grade, navigating the challenges of a transient lifestyle while pursuing his studies.

In 1957, Dr. Rajinder Singh completed his MBBS degree and subsequently undertook a year-long house job at the Government Medical College and Hospital in Patiala.

Driven by his passion for psychiatry, he applied for admission to the Maudsley Institute of Psychiatry in the United Kingdom. Despite being accepted, financial limitations prevented him from seizing the opportunity. Similarly, he was selected for admission to the NIMHANS in Bangalore but again faced financial barriers that prevented him from enrolling.

Although his dream of advanced studies in psychiatry was temporarily deferred, Dr. Rajinder Singh's fervor for the field persisted, underscoring his dogged dedication to his passion, despite obstacles.

After completing his MBBS degree, he began his service as a medical officer (MO) at the Mental Hospital in Amritsar. Under the guidance of Dr. Vidya Sagar, the director-cum-medical superintendent who was renowned in the field of psychiatry and pioneered the establishment of the Outpatient Department (OPD) at the hospital, Dr. Rajinder Singh found inspiration to pursue further education in psychiatry. Initially serving as a non-gazetted MO, he was later promoted to Punjab Civil Medical Services (PCMS) while working at the mental hospital.

In the early 1960s, Dr. Rajinder Singh was posted to the Primary Health Centre in Nadaun, a town in the undivided Punjab's Kangra District, which is now in Hamirpur District in Himachal Pradesh. Despite his modest income, he supported his younger brother's education.

Dr. Vidya Sagar, impressed by Dr. Rajinder Singh's dedicated and compassionate service, requested his return to the mental hospital. Following his tenure at the Primary Health Centre in Nadaun, he was transferred back to the Mental Hospital in Amritsar.

During this period, Dr. Rajinder Singh's family arranged for his marriage. His elder brother, S. Gurbaksh Singh, played a significant role in the matter and personally visited Narnaul, a city in erstwhile Punjab (now in Haryana), to meet the prospective bride. The girl, named Savitri, was also a medical officer posted in Narnaul. S. Gurbaksh Singh was deeply impressed by Savitri and her widowed mother, who had raised her daughter with strong values despite adversities. Learning about Savitri's mother's struggles after losing her husband when Savitri was just a year-and-a-half old, S. Gurbaksh Singh was moved and saw the alliance between Savitri and his brother as a compassionate act in support of those facing hardships. He performed all rituals of the betrothal ceremony there and then in the presence of higher district health authorities and the deputy commissioner. Dr. Rajinder Singh's marriage took place in 1961 while he was stationed at the Mental Hospital in Amritsar. His wife, Dr. Savitri R. Singh, held a higher position in her profession compared to him. To be with his wife after their marriage, Dr. Rajinder Singh requested a transfer to Nangal.

In mid-1962, the couple welcomed a daughter into their family. Around the same time, a national emergency was declared due to the Indo-China War, leading to an urgent need for medical officers in the armed forces. Dr. Rajinder Singh offered his services and joined the armed forces, undergoing training in Hyderabad.

His first posting in the armed forces was as a regimental medical officer in a field ambulance in Pithoragarh, which was part of Uttar Pradesh at the time and is now in Uttarakhand. His duties included providing medical care to troops, conducting inspections, and ensuring sanitation in the regiment. He was impressed by the discipline and decorum maintained by all ranks within the army, noting the absence of political interference. His positive experience led him to pursue a permanent commission in the armed forces, and he qualified for the examination for the same.

During his service, Dr. Rajinder Singh completed advanced courses in psychiatry at the AFMC in Pune and obtained a Diploma in Psychological Medicine (DPM) from Pune University between 1968 and 1970. After successfully clearing both exams, he was posted to Lucknow as a graded specialist in psychiatry in the armed forces. He was later promoted to a classified psychiatrist and eventually became a Senior Advisor in Psychiatry within the armed forces.

During his service, Dr. Rajinder Singh was stationed at various locations, including Lucknow, Chandigarh, Bareilly, and Pathankot. While being posted in Chandigarh, he seized the opportunity to pursue an MD in Psychiatry from the prestigious PGIMER Chandigarh. Following the completion of his MD, he served in Guwahati (Assam) and later was posted in Bareilly, Pathankot, Chandigarh, Calcutta, and Delhi. He retired from the Indian Army in 1991 as a Senior Advisor in Psychiatry, based in Delhi.

Today, Dr. Rajinder Singh is working as a consultant in addiction medicine and running two de-addiction centers. Named Akal Drug De-Addiction Centre, the de-addiction centers are located in Baru Sahib, Himachal Pradesh, and Cheema Sahib, Sangrur, Punjab. He has also published two books titled "Drug Addiction" and 'Be Aware and Beware of Drugs'. Dr. Rajinder Singh's wife was also a graduate of the Medical College in Amritsar. Their son is a lawyer, and their elder daughter, Dr. Neelam Kaur, is an advisor in health and education at Kalgidhar Trust.

Chapter 2

Left Right Left: Days in Uniform

Joining the armed forces meant living by a strict schedule and following orders closely. For Dr. Rajinder Singh, it meant starting the day early with a wake-up call and getting ready quickly. The entire day was planned out, right from training exercises to medical duties.

In tough situations like battles, every second felt important, and soldiers had to focus. Despite the chaos, he found comfort in sticking to the routine he knew so well. As night fell, soldiers gathered around campfires to unwind and share stories. These moments brought them closer together, creating strong bonds. Living by military time wasn't just about following a schedule; it was a way of life. It required perseverance and sacrifice, but it was built on a sense of honor and courage that lasted a lifetime. And for Dr. Rajinder Singh, it was a journey he was proud to be a part of.

After his commission as a captain in the army, his inaugural posting landed him in the rugged terrains of Uttarakhand, in Patharagad district near the volatile China-Nepal-India border. Assigned to a Field Ambulance, Dr. Rajinder Singh found himself thrust into the heart of military life. The canvas of his existence was painted with regimentation: officer mess, residences, all ensconced within tents, emblematic of the era's exigencies.

Amidst the canvas of regimentation, discipline thrived. The rhythm of military life dictated sharp salutes and attention to commanding officers. Every gesture, from entering the mess to addressing superiors, bore the stamp of respect and protocol. It was a world where adherence to hierarchy was sacrosanct, and Dr. Rajinder Singh embraced it with a reverence born of duty.

Despite living in a field environment, cleanliness and discipline were top priorities. When it came to meals, there was a strict routine. The mess head would announce when the food was ready, and everyone would gather to eat. The commanding officer always sat first, followed by the other officers. Only after the commanding officer began eating could the rest start.

This strict adherence to rules was evident even during regimental nights when many officers gathered. When the commanding officer started eating, everyone else followed suit. These practices were all about instilling obedience and discipline in every soldier, ensuring a cohesive and orderly environment even in challenging conditions.

When the commanding officer finished eating, it was a signal for everyone else to stop as well. Even the way the fork and spoon were placed had significance. When they were parallel, it meant the commanding officer was done. During regimental nights, once this signal was given, nobody could continue eating, even if they were still hungry. This strict adherence to protocol ensured respect for authority and maintained discipline within the ranks.

Dr. Rajinder Singh likened the strict discipline and regimentation in the military **to the uncompromising ethos of do or die.** It was a mindset ingrained to ensure obedience and adherence to orders, even in the face of adversity. After his commission, he was posted to various locations, including Jalandhar and Uttar Pradesh, before finally finding himself in a position to pursue his passion for psychiatry. Having already nurtured an interest in the field during civilian life, he seized the opportunity to specialize in psychiatry during his army service.

His application to pursue psychiatry was accepted, leading him to be selected for an Advanced Course in Psychiatry at Pune Medical College. This marked a pivotal moment in his military career, where he could combine his ardor for serving his country with his passion for mental health.

Dr. Rajinder Singh's run into psychiatry continued as he was posted to the AFMC in Pune for selection into a specialist course. During his time there, he pursued a DPM from BJ Medical College, Pune, alongside an advanced course in psychiatry. This period spanned two years and laid the foundation for his specialization in psychiatry.

After completing his DPM, his career took him to esteemed postings as a graded specialist in psychiatry. His first assignment in this role was in Lucknow, followed by a posting at the Command Hospital in Chandigarh, initially situated in Sector 11 before being relocated to Chandi Mandir. He served there from 1972 to 1975, honing his skills and expertise in the field.

During his tenure in Chandigarh, Dr. Rajinder seized the opportunity to further his education by pursuing an MD in Psychiatry from the Post Graduate Institute of Medical Education and Research, Chandigarh (PGIMER). This marked a significant advancement in his profession, as MD programs in psychiatry had recently been introduced, providing him with a comprehensive and in-depth understanding of his chosen specialty.

Dr. Rajinder's post-graduation led him to various hospitals across India, including Pathankot, Chandigarh, Bareilly, Guwahati, Delhi, and Calcutta. These postings offered him diverse experiences and opportunities to contribute his expertise in psychiatry. In 1987, Dr. Rajinder Singh's career reached a significant milestone when he was selected as a Senior Advisor in Psychiatry. At that time, he was stationed in Chandigarh but soon moved to the Command Hospital in Calcutta, where he served for about two to three years before being transferred to Delhi.

His career culminated in his retirement as a Senior Advisor in Psychiatry from the armed forces, with his final posting being at the Delhi Army Hospital in 1991.

Reflecting on his time in the military, Dr. Rajinder Singh found the army life to be fulfilling. He opted for a permanent commission (PC) after initially joining through an emergency commission. His endeavor with the army spanned approximately 30 years, during which he found solace in its structured and disciplined environment.

One of the standout aspects of army life for Dr. Rajinder Singh was its discipline, which was free from the interference of politicians that often plagued civilian medical services. This allowed Dr. Rajinder to focus on his duties without external disruptions, leading to his overall satisfaction with his military career.

Reimagining his military undertaking, Dr. Rajinder Singh acknowledged that initially, he had not considered a career in the armed forces. However, when the nation called for emergency service, he felt compelled to answer. As a psychiatrist, he found his work both fascinating and fulfilling.

Unlike other medical specialties that relied heavily on physical examinations and laboratory tests, psychiatry revolved around listening, analyzing, and diagnosing through conversation. Through counseling and psychotherapy, psychiatrists helped patients navigate their mental health challenges, making sense of what may seem nonsensical at times.

This aspect of psychiatry appealed to Dr. Rajinder Singh; he found joy in simply sitting, listening, and conversing with patients to understand their struggles and offer treatment. It was a departure from the physical demands of other medical specialties, making it both an easy and rewarding profession in his eyes.

Navigating the challenges of dual careers in the military and civil service posed unique obstacles for Dr. Rajinder Singh and his wife, who was also a doctor. Political issues often arose, particularly when his wife faced postings to rural areas while he served in the army. Despite her seniority, political pressure from higher authorities frequently influenced her assignments, resulting in frequent separations and added stress. She had to manage the household and their children's education under these challenging circumstances.

During his annual two-month leave from the army, Dr. Rajinder often advocated for his wife's postings. He recalled an instance when his wife was initially posted to Pathankot but was quickly reassigned to a rural dispensary in Badhani, 15 kilometers away. Determined to address this issue, Dr. Rajinder Singh, in uniform as a colonel, approached Chief Minister Beant Singh.

Despite his efforts to highlight the inconvenience caused by his wife's frequent reassignments, bureaucratic processes often prevailed. Nonetheless, his persistence in advocating for his wife's well-being exemplified his faithfulness to balancing military duty with family life. Dr. Rajinder Singh's wife persevered, ensuring their children received a quality education despite the disruptions caused by their nomadic lifestyle. Her vow to their family's well-being amidst the complexities of dual careers accentuates her force and love for work.

Dr. Rajinder Singh's career as a psychiatrist in the military was marked by professionalism, integrity, and loyalty to his patients' well-being. His devotion to professional ethics and enthusiasm for his patients' well-being serve as an enduring example of the outlook of the human spirit. Dr. Rajinder Singh reflected, "In the face of challenges, our commitment to ethical principles becomes our guiding light." Throughout his career, he embodied this sentiment, navigating the complexities of military service with grace and resolve. As he often said, "In the pursuit of truth and justice, we must remain unyielding, even in the face of adversity." Despite facing pressure, he remained resolute, refusing to compromise his principles for personal gain.

Ultimately, Dr. Rajinder Singh's legacy is best summarized in his own words, "Integrity is the cornerstone of our profession. It is our duty to uphold it, no matter the cost." His story serves as an inspiration that one should not cower under life's greatest challenges.

Chapter 3

Destroyed by Drugs

Nestled in the fertile plains of northern India, Punjab, often referred to as the 'Granary of India', boasts a rich cultural heritage and a legacy of agricultural prosperity. However, beneath this veneer of abundance lies a deep-seated problem that has plagued the state for decades, the insidious scourge of drug abuse. One surely needs to learn more and explore the historical antecedents and contemporary manifestations of the drug crisis in Punjab, shedding light on its multifaceted dimensions and impact on society.

Drug trafficking and massive drug abuse are wreaking havoc in Punjab. The epidemic of substance abuse in the younger generation has assumed alarming dimensions in the state. Experts say that the state may lose an entire generation to rampant abuse of smack, heroin, and synthetic drugs. The people of Punjab demand a strong political will to tackle the drug menace. The problem could be adequately addressed only when seen in a wider socio-economic context.

India is grappling with a growing epidemic of drug abuse, with the number of addicts steadily rising. According to a United Nations report, India has officially registered one million heroin addicts, but unofficial estimates suggest the number could be as high as five million. This alarming trend is particularly concerning in states like Manipur, Mizoram, Nagaland, Himachal Pradesh, Punjab, Haryana, and Western Rajasthan. Among these, Punjab stands out as the most severely affected.

The situation in Punjab is exacerbated by its proximity to porous international borders and well-established drug-trafficking routes, notably the 'Golden Crescent', comprising Iran, Afghanistan, and Pakistan. Drugs infiltrate Punjab not only through the India-Pakistan border but also from neighboring Indian states. Charas and hashish are smuggled into the state via Himachal Pradesh, while opium and poppy husk are trafficked from Rajasthan and Madhya Pradesh.

In July 2018, Punjab sought 'special category' status under the National Health Protection Scheme, portraying itself as the primary victim of Pakistan-sponsored narcotics terrorism. As a border state, Punjab serves not only as a transit point but also as a significant market for drugs.

To understand the roots of Punjab's drug crisis, one must delve into the turbulent history of the region. The 1980s and 1990s were marked by socio-political upheaval, with the rise of militancy and insurgency casting a long shadow over the state. It was during this period that the nexus between drug trafficking, cross-border smuggling, and insurgency began to take root. The porous borders with neighboring countries facilitated the influx of narcotics into Punjab, fueling the burgeoning drug trade.

Furthermore, the Green Revolution hailed as a panacea for agricultural woes, inadvertently exacerbated the drug problem in Punjab. The introduction of high-yield crop varieties and intensive farming practices led to the cultivation of poppy and cannabis, alongside staple crops like wheat and rice. The lure of quick profits enticed many farmers to diversify into illicit cultivation, thereby contributing to the proliferation of narcotics within the state.

Furthermore, a lack of awareness and attention from both the government and society at large has aggravated the issue. Reports indicate that heroin, sourced from Afghanistan at ₹1 lakh per kilogram, traverses through Pakistan and into West Punjab before being smuggled into Indian Punjab, where it fetches a significantly higher price of ₹30 lakh per kilogram. This stark price difference, when compared to other parts of India where it sells for ₹1 crore per kilogram and the international market where it reaches ₹5 crores per kilogram, makes Punjab a prime destination for local youth to fall into the grip of addiction.

According to police sources, heroin, locally known as *chitta* in Punjab, costs addicts no less than Rs 2,000 per day. When addicts exhaust all means to afford their fix, dealers employ a strategy akin to multi-level marketing, offering deals such as sell 10 and get one free. This not only ensures the retention of existing customers but also rapidly expands their clientele base.

Despite being one of India's most prosperous states and the nation's breadbasket, Punjab is grappling with a grave issue that is rapidly escalating, particularly among youth aged between 15 and 25. Shockingly, a survey indicates that 66 percent of school-going students in the state consume *gutka* or tobacco, with one-third of male and one-tenth of female students having experimented with drugs and seven out of 10 college students engaging in drug abuse. After Nagaland, Punjab ranks high in the country for drug abuse, posing a serious threat to the future generation.

(Source: Verma PS. The Drug Menace: Dimensions, Trends and Tribulations in Punjab. Chandigarh: Institute for Development and Communication; 2014.)

The number of deaths attributable to drug abuse is on the rise. The main contributing factors being the use of injections previously used by HIV or HCV-infected individuals, thereby leading to the spread of these diseases within society.

Punjab stands as a pivotal state in India, boasting both strategic and economic significance. Resting between Pakistan, a historical adversary, and the contentious region of Kashmir, it holds a crucial position in India's security landscape. Known as the nation's breadbasket, Punjab plays a vital role in supplying food and manpower to the military—essential components for India's burgeoning economy and defense. However, the state has faced its share of challenges, including a tumultuous period during the 1980s, which was marked by a prolonged insurgency fueled by grievances stemming from the unequal distribution of benefits of the Green Revolution.

Despite efforts to quell unrest, Punjab's economy has faltered over the past decade, worsening issues such as rising drug use and trafficking. This unchecked drug epidemic has provided fertile ground for the convergence of crime and terrorism, posing a significant threat to the hard-won stability post the insurgency. Compounding these challenges is the continued exploitation of identity politics by national and state-level elites, echoing the circumstances that precipitated the previous insurgency. Against this backdrop, the specter of instability looms large over Punjab.

Cut to the present day; Punjab finds itself grappling with the ramifications of decades of neglect and compounding vulnerabilities.

The Punjab Opioid Dependence Survey (PODS) was commissioned by the Union government and conducted in February-April 2015 by the NGO Society for Promotion of Youth and Masses (SPYM) and AIIMS experts. The survey revealed that the state is home to an estimated 860,000 drug addicts, with opioids emerging as the primary substance of abuse. Alarmingly, a significant proportion of these addicts belong to the youth demographic, raising concerns about the future trajectory of Punjab's youth.

The socio-economic implications of the drug crisis are weighty, permeating every facet of Punjab's social fabric. Families are torn asunder, communities are besieged by crime and violence, and the economic vibrancy of the state is undermined by the diversion of resources toward substance abuse. Moreover, the insidious nature of addiction perpetuates a cycle of despair and hopelessness, leaving a trail of shattered dreams and fractured lives in its wake.

Despite concerted efforts to address the drug crisis, Punjab continues to grapple with myriad challenges and controversies. The state's law enforcement agencies have been accused of complicity and corruption, with allegations of collusion between drug traffickers and politicians casting a shadow over efforts to curb the illicit drug trade. Moreover, the stigma associated with addiction has hindered access to treatment and rehabilitation services, adding to the plight of those struggling with substance abuse.

Furthermore, the lack of comprehensive data and research on the prevalence and patterns of drug abuse in Punjab has hampered efforts to formulate evidence-based policies and interventions. While initiatives such as the Punjab Opioid Dependence Survey (PODS) have provided valuable insight into the scale of the problem, there remains a pressing need for ongoing surveillance and monitoring to track trends and guide targeted interventions.

The drug crisis in Punjab represents a complex and entrenched challenge that demands urgent attention and concerted action. While the historical antecedents of the problem are rooted in socio-political upheavals and economic disparities, its contemporary manifestations reflect the need for comprehensive intervention and sustained devotion. Addressing the drug crisis requires a multi-pronged approach, encompassing prevention, treatment, harm reduction, and law enforcement initiatives. Moreover, it necessitates concerted efforts to address the underlying socio-economic determinants of addiction and to foster a culture of empathy as well as support for those grappling with substance abuse. Only through collective action and resolve can Punjab hope to overcome the scourge of drug abuse and reclaim its rightful place as the 'Granary of India'.

Chapter 4

Charitable Heart

Dr. Rajinder Singh came into contact with 'Baba Ji', Sant Baba Iqbal Singh Ji, the president of the Kalgidhar Trust, during the late 1980s when he often visited Baru Sahib and began serving in the medical camps throughout the late 80s and 90s. In the early 2000s, Baba Ji called Dr. Rajinder Singh to share his concerns about the prevalence of drug addiction in Punjab and how it was devastating the youth of the state and the nation. He urged that they must do something to help the young generation of our country.

Baba Ji told him that at their Akal Academies, they are imparting students value-based and spiritual education. It is a combination of modern education with the spiritual component. Their vision lies in transforming students to be of higher moral fiber, and this was the main goal of Baba Iqbal Singh Ji. He wanted these youngsters not to ruin their lives in drug addiction.

Baba Iqbal Singh Ji exhorted Dr. Rajinder Singh to take action to save the youth of the state. Consequently, Dr. Rajinder Singh started a de-addiction center in a gurdwara located in Cheema, near Sunam in Punjab. Cheema is a historical village, the birthplace of Sant Attar Singh Ji Maharaj. Sant Attar Singh Ji was a visionary who made unprecedented contributions to uplift people spiritually. He opened a school for girls at Mastuana in the Malwa region of Punjab in 1906, laid the foundation stone of Banaras Hindu University in December 1914, and envisioned imparting modern education with moral and spiritual values.

When Dr. Rajinder started the de-addiction center, it was just a missionary. He used to go from his hometown, Chandigarh, early on Sundays and then see cases, provide medicines, and come back in the evening. There were no beds, staff, or personnel trained in medical services. Dr. Singh and his small team were managing both the OPD and inpatient cases.

OPD cases were given medicines, while those requiring admission were admitted to the gurdwara, where they lay on the floor. They then trained a few personnel to look after the patients in Dr. Singh's absence. Initially, Dr. Rajinder Singh visited once a week, but these visits gradually became more frequent.

However, when the number of patients increased, help followed. Dr. Rajinder Singh keenly shared what the journey was like, quoting the famous Urdu quote:

میں اکیلا ہی چلا تھا جانب منزل مگر

People came together, and the caravan kept forming

"मैं अकेला ही चला था जानिब-ए-मंज़िल मगर

लोग साथ आते गए और कारवाँ बनता गया"

"Main akela hi chala tha, janib-e-manzil magar, log aate gaye aur Karwan banta gaya."

"I had stepped alone toward the destination

But people kept coming along, making it a caravan"

When Dr. Rajinder Singh started, he was all alone. Then a colleague of his from a de-addiction center in Chandigarh joined him. Thereafter, another psychiatrist from America joined, whom he had met during an academic conference. He expressed the desire to serve the population of Punjab, and he incidentally hailed from District Sangrur. Later, another lady, a German citizen, Mrs. Sarinda, became a part of the team.

What followed were three more members: a doctor from Bombay, a psychiatrist, and another doctor from South India. These people used to help Dr. Singh carry on the work for the indoor patients as well as the OPD.

The gurdwara didn't have any facilities at the start. As the team expanded and the number of patients swelled, Dr. Rajinder Singh recognized the urgent need for dedicated infrastructure. He requested the gurdwara committee and Baba Ji to construct additional premises to accommodate new patients due to spatial constraints within the existing gurdwara premises. This expansion became vital as the demand for services continued to escalate. Through collective effort and devotion, Dr. Rajinder Singh and his team navigated through challenges, ensuring that individuals grappling with addiction received the care and support they desperately required.

This de-addiction center in Cheema is still admitting cases. It is located close to the Gurdwara Janamsthan Sant Attar Singh Ji Maharaj.

The center gradually became a 30-bed hospital for de-addiction cases and is now licensed by the state government. It is one of the biggest centers in the state of Punjab. The special feature for the patients is holistic treatment, which means that they are not only treating patients with modern medication and clinical treatment but are also incorporating the spiritual component along with the traditional treatment. This was an idea that came through Baba Iqbal Singh Ji, who wanted the spiritual component to be incorporated with modern medical treatment.

The team had conducted a pilot study in which the patients were divided into two groups with 60 to 70 patients in each group. One was the experimental group and the other, the control group. In the former, treatment was combined with the spiritual component. While the patients in the control group played cards, watched TV, and followed the regular routine. In the experimental group, the patients engaged in a semi-structured spiritual schedule in addition to regular treatment.

When the performance of the two groups was compared, the results indicated that the withdrawal features of the cases with the spiritual component were better in many areas compared to the traditional group.

Those cases were followed for one year. It was noted that the recovery or the abstention from drugs was comparatively better compared to those who were treated with the traditional treatment.

The two centers—the 30-bed center in Cheema and the 50-bed center in Himachal Pradesh—have been operational since 2016. The centers also comprise facilities for the treatment of female addicts. Notably, The Kalgidhar Trust, having sangat (community) from across the globe, treats patients from England, America, Canada, New Zealand, and other places. At present, they have a young lady from America, a teenage girl, barely 16-17, who is under treatment. Along with the treatment, she is also being educated!

With this approach, the final outcome with these patients is fruitful. A follow-up study of patients in Cheema has been published in the Indian Journal of Social Psychiatry, which confirms that holistic treatment brings better results than the traditional method. "Both are popular de-addiction centers now, but there is some difficulty in the availability of psychiatrists, which will be sorted out in time," Dr. Singh informs.

Numerous dignitaries, including the Health Minister, have visited Akal De-Addiction Centres, acknowledging and commending the exceptional work being carried out. This commendable effort of Dr. Rajinder Singh and his team has carried on for years and will persist further, fueled by the tangible benefits witnessed by the recipients of the treatment. The scourge of drug addiction goes beyond geographical boundaries; it is not solely confined to Punjab or our nation but is a global issue demanding urgent attention. The impact on the youth, who represent our future, is particularly critical, making early intervention imperative.

Dr. Rajinder Singh believes our youth requires education, not drugs. Education serves as a shield, guarding them against the pitfalls of substance abuse. The adage, Prevention is better than cure, applies aptly, as it is easier to stay out of drugs than to come out of them. However, it's imperative to rescue them from the clutches of addiction, steering them toward a drug-free existence. Efforts in the area of de-addiction are earnestly underway with hopes for continued progress in these centers. Challenges will arise, but with willpower, these can be surmounted.

The shortage of mental health professionals is a concern, but there's optimism that it will gradually be addressed, allowing him to deliver services to the best of his abilities. De-addiction is uniquely challenging; it extends beyond mere medical intervention, encompassing social and psychological dimensions as well as impacting families and society at large. Unlike other medical disciplines with more defined boundaries, the effects of addiction ripple widely, touching not only the individual's health but also their familial and societal connections. It's a multifaceted issue that demands a comprehensive approach for effective intervention and support.

Dr. Rajinder Singh highlights the pervasive taboo surrounding de-addiction and rehabilitation centers, which poses significant challenges in patient admission and treatment. The social stigma attached to seeking help for addiction often leads to denial among individuals who require treatment. Even after admission, patients may exhibit reluctance and a strong desire to leave prematurely. Convincing them to stay for the duration of treatment becomes arduous, despite the critical need for comprehensive care. Overcoming this stigma and fostering an environment of acceptance and support is crucial for facilitating effective treatment outcomes and long-term recovery.

Dr. Rajinder Singh emphasizes the demotivation prevalent among patients entering treatment, whose lives are consumed by the relentless pursuit of their next fix. Their priorities are starkly distorted, fixated solely on obtaining drugs, leaving little room for anything else. This grim reality augments the necessity for extensive counseling and management efforts. Addressing addiction is a complex endeavor, requiring a coordinated team effort involving health professionals, counselors, support staff, and security personnel. Despite the inherent challenges, both patients and families exhibit miraculous courage in confronting these obstacles, often yielding positive outcomes. He shows the immense difficulty inherent in addiction psychiatry, given its far-reaching impact on families and society, making it one of the most challenging disciplines within the field of medicine today.

The challenges persist throughout the treatment process, with patients often displaying a strong desire to leave the treatment facility prematurely. Motivating them to stay and complete their treatment is a significant hurdle that institutions must address. Moreover, ensuring regular follow-up post-discharge is paramount, yet many patients fail to adhere to this crucial aspect of their recovery. As a result, relapses are common, leading to suboptimal treatment outcomes.

The success of these treatments hinges heavily on patient compliance and the warrant to follow-up care. Efforts must be intensified to encourage patients to remain engaged in their treatment and adhere to post-discharge protocols to enhance the likelihood of sustained recovery.

The challenge of treatment non-compliance often stems from a variety of factors, including family issues and underlying personality struggles. Practitioners recognize the potential of holistic approaches to yield more favorable outcomes when compared to traditional methods.

This holistic approach integrates modern medical practices with a spiritual component, emphasizing the importance of regular prayer, meditation, and spiritual practices. By addressing not only the physical but also the spiritual aspects of addiction, patients are guided toward a deeper understanding of their condition and the path to recovery. The infusion of spirituality serves as a catalyst for evolution, fostering a sense of purpose and connection that complements the therapeutic process, ultimately contributing to improved treatment outcomes.

Dr. Rajinder Singh emphasized the importance of establishing a strong moral foundation to guide individuals away from the pitfalls of substance abuse. When individuals deviate from moral values, introspection, and realignment with ethical principles become essential for their rehabilitation. Alongside treatment, efforts must also focus on preventing substance abuse and recognizing the complexity of the issue. The invaluable support provided by altruistic trusts is instrumental in overcoming the numerous challenges faced by the de-addiction centers, without which the task would be significantly daunting. In addressing substance abuse among patients, particularly youth, comprehensive strategies encompassing awareness, prevention, treatment, and moral guidance are essential for fostering lasting recovery and well-being.

Dr. Singh also believes that emphasis should be placed on preventive measures. Prevention is not solely the responsibility of psychiatrists or mental health professionals; parents also play a crucial role. During the formative years of childhood, children should be encouraged to receive moral education and be trained in ethical as well as spiritual values. Instilling spirituality in childhood may help deter distractions later in life, compared to those who haven't received such training. The effectiveness of treatment greatly hinges on the preventive measures. Additionally, the availability of drugs is a significant factor. Despite the government's efforts, drugs are easily available, posing a challenge. If drugs are easily accessible, individuals are more likely to indulge. Addressing this availability issue is crucial. Solely relying on de-addiction centers cannot effectively tackle this problem. This is his solid viewpoint on the situation.

Unless there's a concerted effort to emphasize preventive measures and instill values in youth, particularly starting from childhood, substance abuse cannot be curbed. The pivotal roles of parents and teachers cannot be overstated in this regard. Commencing preventive measures during childhood is paramount rather than waiting until addiction takes hold. Without adequate training in moral and ethical principles, achieving positive outcomes becomes increasingly challenging. While de-addiction centers play a role in reducing addiction cases, the overall outcome for patients often remains unsatisfactory. Moreover, the escalating number of youth succumbing to drugs stresses the inadequacy of solely relying on de-addiction efforts. Effectively addressing drug availability demands strict adherence to regulations governing narcotic substances. Additionally, prioritizing preventive measures should involve imparting ethical values and discouraging drug use despite its availability. By steadfastly pursuing these objectives, better outcomes can be anticipated compared to merely depending on de-addiction centers. It's essential to recognize that this issue extends beyond borders, necessitating collective global efforts to safeguard youth from the perils of addiction. Each individual bears a responsibility to contribute to this noble cause, working tirelessly to shield the younger generation from devastation and despair.

Dr. Singh firmly believes in the unique approach of blending spirituality with treatment for addiction. While most centers adhere to traditional methods, his unit stands apart by integrating spiritual practices into the recovery process. This innovative approach aims to address the deeper dimensions of addiction and facilitate holistic healing. By incorporating spirituality, patients are provided with a comprehensive framework for change and growth. He and his team meticulously measure the success of patients treated with this holistic approach, recognizing the impact it can have on their strive for recovery. Their pioneering effort has set a new standard in addiction treatment, demonstrating the effectiveness of a multidimensional approach that encompasses both medical and spiritual aspects.

Dr. Rajinder Singh advocates the importance of clinical research in understanding treatment outcomes, particularly in assessing patient abstinence and relapse rates. In the context of opiate addiction, the center administers a medication known as buprenorphine-naloxone tablet, which he asserts is highly effective but often subject to misconceptions. Despite its efficacy, government regulations, and familial concerns pose significant barriers to its accessibility. Families sometimes hold misguided beliefs, insisting that patients abstain completely from all drugs, including those crucial for managing opiate addiction. This attitude impedes access to safe and effective treatment options. He stresses the necessity of making such medications readily available to patients, emphasizing their importance in harm reduction and preventing relapse into more harmful substances like opium derivatives. However, stringent government controls limit access to these medications, necessitating collaboration and advocacy efforts to ensure patients receive the comprehensive care they need.

In private practice, psychiatrists are unable to dispense medication directly. Dr. Rajinder Singh emphasizes the importance of providing certain drugs, especially for opiate addiction, which constitutes a significant portion, around 40 to 50 percent, of total cases. Despite encountering various challenges, gradual resolution seems plausible.

The government is actively involved, particularly in the area of rehabilitation, as mentioned by the Health Minister, who announced the establishment of a vocational center in Patiala. This initiative aims to provide employment and training to aid in rehabilitation efforts. Addressing the root causes of relapse, such as idleness, is crucial. Dr. Rajinder Singh stresses the importance of work, considering it as a form of medicine. Individuals who are fully engaged in constructive activities are less likely to resort to drugs. This heightens the significance of keeping occupied in the recovery process.

The staff of de-addiction centers conducts family sessions every fortnight, interacting with family members, such as spouses, mothers, and other relatives, and offering counseling as part of their holistic management approach. These family sessions play a crucial role in dispelling misconceptions about medication. Despite their best efforts, some misconceptions persist, particularly the expectation that individuals should be completely drug-free upon leaving the de-addiction centers. Understanding the chronic nature of addiction, they emphasize the necessity of long-term follow-up, spanning not just weeks or months but possibly years.

However, some struggle to comprehend this reality, expecting swift recovery within one or two months of admission, which is unrealistic, given the complexity and enduring nature of addiction. Reforming and transforming individuals with addiction is an arduous task, requiring significant effort. Additionally, many patients face stigma and mental health issues, which may persist even if they do not relapse, leading to further challenges in their recovery path.

The fear of societal stigma often deters individuals from seeking admission to de-addiction centers, as they worry about the potential damage to their reputation within their families and communities. This taboo surrounding addiction acts as a significant barrier to accessing treatment. However, it's crucial to emphasize that without seeking treatment, individuals cannot overcome their addiction. Those struggling with addiction require specialized care in de-addiction centers to effectively address their condition.

Additionally, there's a pressing need for preventive measures to curb the onset of addiction, particularly among vulnerable youth. Early intervention through preventive counseling plays a pivotal role in educating individuals about the dangers of substance abuse and empowering them to make informed choices. By prioritizing prevention efforts, we can mitigate the societal impact of addiction and promote healthier lifestyles, adhering to the adage that 'prevention is indeed better than cure'.

Treatment presents numerous challenges, yielding unsatisfactory outcomes, particularly among our rural population, who struggle to afford the exorbitant costs. The expense primarily stems from the necessity to maintain a substantial cadre of mental health professionals, all of whom rightfully expect compensation for their services.

Reflecting on Dr. Rajinder Singh's extensive experience treating countless patients, particularly youth grappling with addiction, one might wonder about its toll on his own mental well-being. Surprisingly, rather than detracting from his mental health, this enriches it. He shares each encounter and provides invaluable insights into the intricate pathways leading individuals into the perilous realm of addiction.

Instead of feeling burdened by this knowledge, it empowers him. He gains a deeper understanding of the underlying motivations driving individuals toward substance abuse. This expanded perspective not only enhances his own mental character but also equips him with invaluable knowledge to guide others away from similar pitfalls.

Foremost among these lessons is an understanding of what not to do. Armed with this knowledge, he can effectively communicate preventive measures to patients, steering them clear of the dangerous path toward addiction.

As he reflects on his career beginnings in a mental hospital, he recognizes the evolution in the field of addiction treatment. While challenges persist, the availability of resources and understanding has vastly improved. With each patient, he is reminded of the transformative impact that compassionate and informed care can have in combating addiction.

The Punjab Mental Hospital in Amritsar was once steeped in taboo, with the prevailing notion that those who ventured into psychiatry were somehow half-mad. While this stigma has somewhat diminished over time, traces of it still linger. Despite the nature of Dr. Rajinder Singh's work, he has never felt that it has negatively impacted his mental health. On the contrary, he proudly shares it enriches his well-being and fosters personal growth.

Engaging with patients has been enlightening, one that has significantly contributed to Dr. Rajinder Singh's emotional and psychological development. Rather than feeling emotionally drained or overwhelmed, he finds himself experiencing a sense of fulfillment and purpose. Each interaction serves as a learning opportunity, further enhancing his understanding of human behavior and mental health dynamics.

Indeed, the notion of psychiatry being associated with madness or abnormality is nothing more than a superstition, a remnant of a bygone era. He recalls a time when diseases like leprosy and sexually transmitted infections were also shrouded in taboo. However, societal attitudes have evolved over time, largely due to widespread education and awareness efforts.

Similarly, mental illness is gradually shedding its stigma, albeit not entirely eradicated. Psychiatry is now recognized as a valuable and sought-after specialty, with increasing competition for admission into psychiatric programs. This shift in perception underlines the growing acknowledgment of the crucial role mental health professionals play in promoting overall well-being.

In essence, the decreasing taboo associated with mental health issues signifies progress in our collective understanding and acceptance of diverse health challenges. As we continue to prioritize mental health awareness and education, Dr. Rajinder paves the way for a more inclusive and supportive society, where individuals feel empowered to seek help without fear or shame.

Indeed, societal attitudes toward various health issues, including mental illness and addiction, have undergone substantial revision over time. While drug addiction was virtually non-existent a few decades ago, it has now become a pressing concern, demanding concerted efforts from governments, NGOs, and the general public alike. The youth, in particular, are vulnerable to the allure of drugs, amidst the complexities of adolescence marked by exploration and risk-taking.

As an observer of these developments, Dr. Rajinder Singh has grappled with understanding the underlying causes of addiction. Often, patients' narratives reveal a poignant truth—the impact of trauma and loss on their lives. For instance, the tragic loss of a loved one can trigger immense emotional turmoil, leading some individuals to seek solace in drugs as a coping mechanism.

However, it is imperative to recognize that resorting to drugs as a means of stress relief is not only detrimental but also perpetuates a cycle of harm. Education and awareness are crucial in promoting healthier coping mechanisms, such as music, nature walks, exercise, and meditation, as alternatives to substance abuse.

Reflecting on his experiences treating patients, one poignant case stands out. In Cheema, a young patient was brought to the center by his father, despite his reluctance to seek treatment. The conflict between father and son, one urging admission while the other resisting, epitomized the complexities of addiction intervention. Ultimately, with the assistance of their staff, the patient was admitted to the de-addiction center and received comprehensive treatment, including medication, counseling, and spiritual practices, like prayers and meditation. Over time, he experienced gradual improvement and stabilization.

These encounters highlight the multifaceted nature of addiction and the challenges inherent in its treatment. The patients also highlight the potential for positive change and recovery through compassionate care and holistic intervention. By addressing the root causes of addiction and providing support tailored to individual needs, we as a society can empower individuals to embark on a journey of recovery and healing. But the patient remained there for about six weeks, and then he eloped. He absconded from the patient care because he wanted to go home.

The father of the patient was fed up because he had lost his elder son due to drugs. But then he was brought again by the father and other relatives; he was readmitted. This time, the resistance was not much. The same treatment started, and he also participated in meditation and other prayers.

*Dr. Rajinder Singh being greeted after commissioning in the
Army Medical Corps*

Dr. Rajinder Singh being awarded- MBBS degree during convocation

Dr. Rajinder Singh during a conference on Drug Abuse in Delhi 1990

Addressing a talk on anti depressant at Command Hospital Calcutta, 1989

One with Nature

Bidding farewell to a colleague at Command Hospital Chandigarh, 1987

Senior officer visits the psychiatry wing of Command Hospital Chandigarh, 1988

Dr Rajinder Singh with his class Xth classmates 1947-48

During an exercise in JMO course, Army Medical Corps

Drug awareness and education webinar, after the award of London Book of World Record, in 2020

Lifetime achievement award for being a crusader against drug addiction, by Grey Shades 2023

London Book of World Records 2023, Dr. Rajinder Singh with the students of Akal Academy Baru Sahib

Being greeted at the Prominent Punjabi Award 2024 by the speaker of Punjab Legislative Assembly S. Kultar Singh Sandhwan

Prominent Punjabi Award 2024, being Presented by S. Kaultar Singh Sandhwan, speaker of Punjab Legislative Assembly

Dr. Rajinder Singh, with S.Harpal Singh and Dr. BNS Walia

During the release of Dr. Rajinder Singh's book - 'Gems of Wisdom on World Book Day 23rd April, 2024

Dr. Rajinder Singh with Smt. Amar Kulwant Singh and Shri Vivek Atray, former IAS during a Q&A session on World Book Day 23rd April, 2024

Interaction at Rotary Club Chandigarh, Saving youth from drugs, Oct 2024

Happy New Year — 1998
"Avoid Self destruction

Hitherto up to this year of ninety seven
Boy which we all are even (eq?
Retired, matured with time and age,
Turn to our history and every page.
We fulfilled hope of Rev. Papa ji
Broke Shackles of Sheer Poverty
While his Ship is younder the Beach.
Two of his wishes are yet to reach.
So refresh our vow, to live at par
Remain united as we are
With spirit of brotherhood and sacrifice.
To keep away the Demon Avarice
Money, Property and material means
Peoples Jealousy and other genes
Of callous hatred and dismity
& Ever remember Papa ji's dignity
Be five Pandos of Present Century"

Bauji

To Dr Rajinder Singh
Chandigarh.

Copy

14.11.69

Jamnagar House
New Delhi

11/11/69

Dear Raj,

Your of 7th Nov. to hand just now when I come back from village, Amit is enjoying Diwali there with other members. Avoiding Papa ji etc. He could not write to you after visiting Poona as he was perfectly alright and remained busy with buffalos feeding. He is very happy. I think you are not in touch with village and other affairs or I write in details. I doubt my letters containing full accounts have not reached you.

<u>Papa ji & Village Brothers</u>, After great consideration it was decided that the family can prosper if the village is developed, & for that Papa ji's presence is necessary. Power Tube-wells to be installed for making land more productive. So in May & June I visited village & saw the authorities. Applications given, Rs 30/- spent on the project. Then I wrote you to send application for giving permission. Your application has been received. Then Rahimabad developments come in our way. I saw the minister

9/7/72

Greenland Dolmuji.

Dearest Paramjit and Riju.

H.S.S.Y.

I have dropped you another letter, you might have received. The affairs of village are OK. but Bhabiji is not still normal although medicine (desi) has been brought from Delhi & used. The main trouble is that she does not take rest. Her brain is too active to take rest. Day & night she keep herself busy doing & undoing the things and continue speaking with things and talking at night while doing work and thus recapitulating the past happenings.

She is not happy generally and sometimes weeps but

Happy new year. 1998

On your visit, we offer hearty cheer;
    On the ushering of this new year.
Oh Couple of diamonds, nice you are;
    you awaken our spirit and open heart.

Heritage of Sikhism, you carry with you;
    Drench our thirst like drops of dew.
Even your shadow, has magic tact;
    Whosoever see you, is impressed in fact.
What to talk of, mature People;
    'Right Path' you show, even to supple;
Matchless example, we watched in 'Amrita';
    None else it results; except Ma and Pa.
In such tender age, she recited 'Rehras'
    well versed in 'Gurbani' & performed 'Ardas'

Oh dear Couple, we most you like,
    Neelam our gem. Davinder our pride
We wish you both, within core of heart;
    Ever you come, but never to hast.

        Thus we wish this, The 'Ninety Eight';
        Rather all the years in our fate.

                            Gur hashasth Sj
To Couple of DIAMONDS   Rajinder Sing
    Baru Sahib.   with all Bhartina
    Camp: Chandigarh.   family

HAPPY NEW YEAR

Oh dear young,
        year has sung,
    its own songs
        Burry its wrongs..

With fresh year,
        New hopes,dear,
    with new life,
        With new smile.-

Fulfil the goal,
        Play your role,
    with such thunder,
        World may wonder.-
    Without aims rootless,
        Without Achievement fruitless,
    Remember your aim,
        Make your name.-
    Send we all,
        New years call,
    Neelam, Papu Mother,
        Amarjit,you, other.
    Happy New Year,
        Others all year,
    In our fate,,
        not only Fifty-eight..

Dr. Rajinder Singh, — *Pride of family*   Gurbakhash Singh
Faridkot..   Delhi
                                            Dated 1.1.68.

My dearest Reji

I have joined
to day & is here. Papu Satya
& Vissa Singh are with me. in
this desert — The place is
horrible in all respects. I am
quite upset — I will try to
[in this Kauli] live for 10 days or so.
Nothing is available —

You should request the
authorities to allot a house
at Lucknow so that at
we may shift to that
place & get our children
admitted in good School

No School at K aule.
What a place.
Papu Reports to you
with all Love

Yours own
Santu

PS
I left Neelam & Mattapee
weeping at Faizabad
as it was not possible
to bring them here
at all costs. R

<u>On the new year 1991.</u>

Every year when it ends;
    Papa,'s memory, along it sends.
His novel and marvellous performance;
    which left the family, constant fragrance
A great builder, a great tiller;
    from tinny stones, he made a piller.
His Contributions turned family fame,
    Shouldn't we also keep his name?
Tread his path and thus we go;
    Let us then if wish we So.
Life we live, which lived by none
    our curse and purse be always coming
He wished us all to annually meet—
    For news, reviews to hearts neat
Let us step towards his light;
    The only penacea for life's delight.
with all these words, I wish new year,
    Not this year, but years' year.
Not only this year of Ninety one;
    But all the years yet to come.

Col Dr Rajinder Singh.
Savitri R Singh
   Delhi Cantt.

      Ever yours
      Gurbakhash Singh,

Wish to send you,

The lines few,

On this year new:

You remember too,

What we are to do,

Rise from common lot,

Stage,where World rot.

All lesson we gather,

is"to live for other"

Eahh for all,all for each,

Ways of progress,thus teach.

History says so,

Men come men go,

But those,do stay,

whose part of play

is strange and great,

Need I them narrate?

Ours is strange Family,

We rose like that tree,

Whish grows on the rock,

True, if we take stock.

We should nourish it more,

More , more and more.

It may grow very high,

Outshoot the world,touch sky,

To reahh this aim,

Way is simple and plain.

Firstly,we love each and all,

To live in each others heart.

Secondly,We remember for century,

To give progress to Family.

New Year's Greetings.

something special in this year,

      To tell you, oh my dear,

of long I wished to disclose

About our family by angle close.

Turn its pages, before sixty years,

      Troubles, illiteracy, labour and tears,

Life was passed in Kacha Hut,

      Rags to wear with common cut.

A great man appeared in it,

      Who made this family to live fit.

Depressed of poverty and loathsome phase,

      Many throes he faced with grace.

Winters he passed without warm clothes,

      In surroundings, he earned vast loath.

He resolved to prove himself versatile,

      By changing the family to modern style.

To put in it doctors and engineer,

      He never took rest, till, oh dear.

For sixty years struggle, it does matter,

      Careers he made five sons and brothers.

He changed the pattern of family style,

      How strange in his own life.

He reached success slow by slow,

      But appearing humble with poor show.

He knit the family of marvelous ties,

      Which you see now before your eyes.

To-day we are, what he wished us,

      Why not cherish, his respect in us?

End of a great epoch.

My dearest Raj & Amarjit,

Writing this letter with rolling tears with deeply moved heart to learn about the death of Mata ji who was a extra ordinary personality.

The career made of dear Amarjit having none else to support, reflects her great acemen. She has followed our great father. They are the founder of our modern family. Being for sighted, having fire in heart to accomplish their high aims of life. Mata ji has excelled in respect that she was great administrator, behaving in family descipline.

Reply 31.1.70

1/1/70

Dearest Rajindar,

I am sending you the new year greetings alongwith the Programme of the year 1970.

I am in receipt of your letter of new year greetings also carrying news that Neelam & Pspr had been to village to see you. This is very good. Pspr also wrote me about their good time having spent there.

Surindra's ginger to village, his stay upto 31-1-70. Similarly Mohinder is leaving for one month stay at village. I shall be also here on 25th & will remain for 3 days. We shall hold meeting on the living issues & also perform some Job towards installing Tube well & electrifying the house. It would be very very good had you been

Proceedings of the 2nd Meeting of Bhamrah Ever-Welfare
Corporation held at village Doburjee, on 24th December,
1967, at 8.30 P.M. till 4.30 A.M. of 25th December, 1967.
-.-

The following members were present:-

1) S. Bhagat Singh — *President*
2) S. Harbans Singh — *Gen.Secretary,*
3) S. Gurbakhash Singh
4) S. Rajinder Singh — *Convener*
5) S.Mohinder Paul Singh — *Director of village affairs*
6) S. Paramjit Singh — *financial Secretary.*

AND

7) Smt. Kartar Kaur
8) Mrs. Devinder Kaur

Absent

1. S.Surinder Singh. Chief Auditor
2 S. Avtar Singh. Director of inspections.
3 S. Prithpal Sgh. Advisor Agri. affairs

AGENDA

1. Five Year Plans of Bhamrah Ever-Welfare Corporation.

2. Problem of cooking meals for the parents at village Doburjee.

3. Future of Mohinder Paul Singh.

4. Increase of Joint Fund.

5. Drafting of constitution of Bhamrah Ever-Welfare
   Corporation (abbreviated as B.E.W.C.)

6. Maintenance allowance to Bibi Jee (Smt. Harcharan Kaur).

Item No.1 - Five Year Plan.

It was decided that/first Five Year Plan for the progress of

B.E.W.C. will be effective from 1st April, 1968 to 31st March,

1973. The following progress will be made:-

1. Installation of tube-well at village Doburjee.

2. Increase of agricultural land to 15 acres i.e. 3 acres
   in a year.

3. Setting up of a fruit-garden in fields near the well.

4. Setting up of a kitchen garden in Haveli attached to
   the residence at the village.

5. Self-cultivation to take effect from 1st April,1968.

6. Purchase of a car during the Plan.

7. Joint-Fund to be collected at the rate of Rs 500/- per
   month, thus amounting to Rs 30,000/- in the first Five
   Year Plan, on 50:50 basis by (uncle) S. Harbans Singh
   and (father) S.Bhagat Singh.

   Uncle Ji here suggested that he should be allowed to

   think over this and thereafter he will be able to say

   whether he could contribute towards Joint-Fund or not.

   In the meanwhile, Contributions shall be made by dear

My dearest Rajji,

Thanks... the envelope containing... 1st week of Feb — I wrote 3–4 letters & brother at Delhi. But he never cared to reply... mother felt very ill — ... suddenly... I send them telegrams... to help is all gone with the world. He has been promising help in Feb but never wrote anything much. When he has not taken... to his coming in my... das not arise — I... away that's why one met... I get upset & seek their help — Rest assured in future I would always avoid bothering him — to their troubles... mimi... You want us to... not her. Parkki bali — the way in which... parkki bali — home never behaved with us — no chance of visiting them — Ikaki a... chapter — no more opening such...

Happy New Year.

Bravo bravo, all of you,

    A herald of the year's new

We are successful for all the year

    Credit goes to unity, Oh dear

Day by day now shines our family,

    Tube well, thrasher, and electricity,

If unity remains like so,

    United like hand & globe

Certainly we create thunder

    Seeing this, the world wonder.

For solid & successful life,

    Now we enter in new life.

With blessing of the Diety,

    We have founded "Society"

A great show, is up now

    Life means to develope, how?

Simple to answer it all,

    "United we stand, divided we fall".

In the years yet to come,

    With our aims we shall run.

This my wish of the new year,

    To follow up in other years,

Not this year of 1971 Seventy-one

    But all the years yet to come.

. . . .

1. Dr. Rajinder Singh.
2. S. Surrender Singh
3. S. Mahendra Paul Singh
4. S. Paramjit Singh.

Gurbakhash — Delhi.

1. 1. 1971.

On 15th death anniversary of Papa ji.

Surprised enough, Oh dear brother
    Absentee Pammy, Pamel and Swinder.
Think a little, Past and now
    Your status who made and how?
Sixty year ordeal, lies behind it,
    Lived without comforts to make you fit.
Think more, who was he?
    None else, dear except Papa ji.
Have you ever seen any like him
    Changed the family and made us you
How should we cherish in our life
    No other way than keep him alive
By following his advice as true sons do
    Some of it today we review
To remain united' come what may,
    'To yearly meet' how far we away,
Think, are we honest and true to him,
    If so then today why attendence thin
By this 'You defy the common say
    'Where is the will there is the 'way'
I fear, in future this ugly plight
    Blood in you, may turn white
Then what people say in times to come
    An example, father was betrayed by Sons
Do you remember, to people his Sermons
    God has given him five 'Servants'
'Panj Piaras' recorded it, in his Poetry
    And you are ousting him from memory.
If such is the reward in Selfish return
    Then damn the world, life be burn
No, in worlds bickerings you are at best
    How you perform Duty at level best
So keep your Motto engraved in word.
    Our Brotherhood' marvellously shine in world

Gar bakhash Singh
21st June 1992

Happy New Year 1994.

On   this occasion, again we recall
        I wish this year happy to all;
Though physicall not,yet for ever
        Live in mind, our respected father,
all you remember his life's philosphy
        He showed us path, to live in unity;
so, role you play, How its nice
        To follow his steps and worthy advice;
Bravo, Bravo, on this score,
        I wish in future more and more ,
He struggled hard to make us reach
prosperity of Family to this began
        He made us all, what we seem;
        In our status per his dream
It behoves us all, to live for him;
        And bear the troubles on our skin,
First to glow the Unity's flame
        Second to keep alive his name;
Never to forget, " each for all",
        "United we ries, divided we fall;
Our father's wish we all do,
        An yearly meet ,we start too;
To remove the mis-givings, what may cloud,
        For smooth life, clear the doubts;
so essential a step, that there is none,
        with painy foot how one can run;
In last year, Unity was put to test,
        We braved the old, as per Pappy's Text,
Had we follow the " the yearly meet"
        we kept the family' clean and neat;

An ode on retirement

To day I recall men of honour,
    who Passed the world with wise and glamour
Aristotle, Sandi Plato and Socrate,
        Gari Baldi, Lincoln, Rouseau and Bocrate;
Smith, Shelly, Keat and Boyron,
        Wordsworth, Pigou, Ruskin & Rayon,
Vollaire, Dupeex, Tulsi and Gandhi
        Goethe, Kant and great Lasky
Ram, krishan, Vyas and Karan;
        And many others countless to learn.
Sarwan, Sohrab, and Guru Gobind
        All their virtues, combine in 'my jind'
All are wealth of Past century
        Now talk of a man of this ending century
After reading, it behoves on you
        To tell his name in second' few.
An angel on earth, devoted to humanity
        Sobriety, fraternity and Society
Gentle, noble, humble and simple;
        Countless virtues, in him do twinkle.
Devotion to cause, his life entail,
        Treats his patients like Nightingale.

The Akal Drug De-Addiction Centres have a special spiritual person, known as the divinity teacher, who imparts this spiritual education and ensures everyone attends these discourses. After about two to three weeks, a noticeable shift occurs in their mindset; the patient becomes remarkably positive, expressing confidence in the recovery. This positive change is further fueled by active participation in indoor and outdoor activities, instilling a sense of hope and purpose.

As the patient and family regularly visited the center every fortnight or month, exceptional progress was noticed. His improvement was so significant that it even impacted their familial dynamics. Witnessing the patient's recovery, the family bestowed upon him the symbolic gesture of *'chadar pani'*, signifying his newfound responsibility as the husband of his late brother's widow.

In addition to reclaiming familial responsibilities, the younger brother found stability in his personal and professional life. He secured employment and even started a family of his own, experiencing the joys of fatherhood. Yet, his odyssey does not end there; he embarked on a mission of social service, advocating for others who are reluctant to seek help for their addiction. Despite facing resistance, he remained steadfast in his responsibility to bring them to the de-addiction center, recognizing the transformative power of recovery and the importance of extending a helping hand to those in need.

He's now acutely aware of the pain endured by individuals struggling with addiction, as well as the anguish experienced by their parents and loved ones. Consequently, he continues his altruistic service, leveraging his own work to inspire others toward recovery. His credibility and personal transformation make him a persuasive advocate, as patients are more inclined to heed his advice over that of their families or friends.

This phenomenon is rare yet immensely impactful. The de-addiction center has witnessed the emergence of several individuals who, having successfully completed treatment and maintained sobriety through regular follow-ups, now dedicate themselves to assisting others on the path to recovery. Their firsthand experience lends credibility to their efforts and serves as a light of hope for those still struggling.

Among these wonderful stories is that of an alcoholic who, despite holding a government position in the electricity department, spiraled into alcoholism and promiscuity, leading to the dissolution of his marriage and contracting HIV as well as HCV. Remarried to a widow who supported his rehabilitation, he faced numerous relapses, enduring a staggering 31 admissions to the center.

However, a transformative shift occurred during his final admission, marked by his active engagement in spiritual practices and adherence to the path of recovery. Upon discharge, he continued to attend follow-up appointments diligently, gradually reclaiming his health and vitality. His progress culminated in a moment of astonishment for the medical staff when he arrived for a consultation unaided, a stark contrast to his previous arrivals in wheelchairs or stretchers. Witnessing his transition was a source of immense joy and validation, highlighting the transformative power of strength of mind. Despite the challenges posed by alcoholism, his commitment to recovery ultimately led to his discharge from the center, an exemplification of his triumph over adversity. How a long-term alcoholic and debased person metamorphosed into a sober and baptized individual dressed in a turban; the story featured in Tribune exclusive feature dated 6th September 2024 under the title, "De-addiction Centre at Cheema Sangrur doing yeoman service."

While the internet lacks records of his extensive admissions, his hard work serves as a poignant reminder of the enduring nature of addiction and the tenacity required to overcome it. Though alcoholism may present lifelong challenges, his story illustrates that sustained effort and support can lead to change and lasting recovery.

As he fades from the center's radar, presumably enjoying a life of restored health and purpose, his story remains a witness to the transformative potential of compassionate care and the indomitable human spirit. Indeed, these narratives of redemption are both captivating and inspiring, underscoring the impact of holistic addiction treatment on individual lives and broader communities alike. Dr. Rajinder Singh says there are many other examples of successful happy endings.

Selfless service is the antidote to drugs, a belief deeply ingrained in the ethos of *seva*, or voluntary service. In Sikh 'Ardas', the prayer concludes with the invocation of Guru Nanak's name, invoking a spirit of eternal optimism and the collective welfare of humanity. Yet, preceding this, there's a plea for divine blessings: *'Waheguru, menu samat baksho. Simran te seva da daan baksho'*. This translates into a request for spiritual strength through meditation and service, emphasizing their pivotal roles in leading a righteous life.

This spiritual perspective accentuates the power of thought and perception in shaping one's reality. As the saying goes: If you change the way you look at things, the things you look at change.

Indeed, our thoughts dictate our words, which in turn influence our actions. Thus, fostering a positive mindset and attitude is paramount, and spiritual orientation serves as a guiding light in this endeavor.

Central to this philosophy is the recognition of the transformative potential of words. Words possess the ability to uplift, inspire, and heal. By altering one's thoughts, words, and ultimately actions, one can change their life's trajectory. Hence, the emphasis on spiritual teachings and the cultivation of a supportive environment conducive to positive growth matters.

The importance of holistic lifestyle changes cannot be overstated. While medication plays a crucial role in treating addiction, addressing broader aspects of an individual's life is equally essential. Factors such as social connections, dietary habits, physical activity, and overall well-being contribute significantly to the recovery.

Ultimately, the goal is not merely abstinence from drugs but the holistic modification of the individual. This process entails nurturing a healthy mindset, fostering supportive relationships, and embracing positive lifestyle choices. By attending to these various facets of an individual's life, de-addiction centers strive to instill lasting change and empower individuals to lead fulfilling, drug-free lives.

In essence, the expedition toward recovery is multifaceted and requires a comprehensive approach that addresses the spiritual, emotional, and physical dimensions of wellness. Through a combination of spiritual guidance, therapeutic interventions, and lifestyle modifications, individuals can embark on a path of healing and personal growth. While the road may be challenging, the rewards of a transformed life are immeasurable.

In the context of addiction treatment, service plays a vital role in supporting individuals in their bid for recovery. Whether through volunteering at de-addiction centers, participating in support groups, or providing mentorship to those in need, service brings a sense of purpose and meaning to both the giver and the recipient.

Service extends beyond the individual to the broader community and society at large. It is a collective endeavor aimed at promoting the well-being of all individuals and fostering a culture of compassion and empathy. By engaging in acts of service, individuals not only contribute to the greater good but also experience personal growth and fulfillment.

Moreover, service fosters a sense of connection and belonging, which are essential elements of recovery. By engaging in acts of service, individuals form bonds with others who share similar experiences and challenges. These connections provide a support network that encourages accountability and growth.

Service also serves as a form of self-care, allowing individuals to shift their focus away from their own struggles and redirect their energy toward helping others. By helping others, individuals gain a sense of empowerment and control over their lives, which can be instrumental in overcoming addiction.

Furthermore, service promotes social responsibility and civic engagement, encouraging individuals to actively participate in the betterment of their communities. By working together toward a common goal, individuals develop a sense of pride and ownership in their community, which can have a positive impact on their overall well-being.

Dr. Rajinder Singh says he believes that service is a powerful tool in the fight against addiction. By embracing the principles of *seva* and dedicating oneself to the service of others, individuals can find purpose, connection, and healing on their venture to recovery.

Service not only benefits the individual but also contributes to the greater good, creating a ripple effect of positive change that extends far beyond the individual. He often quotes the following lines enshrined in the Sri Guru Granth Sahib about seva or volunteering:

ਸੇਵਾ ਕਰਤ ਹੋਇ ਨਿਹਕਾਮੀ

ਤਿਸ ਕਉ ਹੋਤ ਪਰਾਪਤਿ ਸੁਆਮੀ

- Sri Guru Granth Sahib 286

One who performs selfless service, without thought of reward, shall attain their Lord and Master.

Financial adversities have been a persistent challenge since the inception of addiction treatment centers. Even today, the burden of financial strain continues to weigh heavily. Securing the necessary funds to sustain operations remains a daunting task, particularly in light of the exorbitant costs associated with employing mental health professionals.

The disparity in remuneration between psychiatrists and other medical specialists exacerbates the financial strain. Psychiatrists often command significantly higher salaries, making it increasingly difficult for addiction treatment centers to afford their services. This financial hurdle draws the broader issue of stigma surrounding mental health, as psychiatry remains a less desirable field due to societal misconceptions.

Furthermore, the economic landscape in rural areas presents additional challenges. Limited financial resources constrain the ability of addiction treatment centers to provide affordable care to those in need. Concessions and free services are often necessary to accommodate individuals facing financial hardship, further straining the center's financial viability.

Despite these financial constraints, addiction treatment centers remain steadfast in their work providing essential services to their communities. However, the pressure to maintain financial sustainability often leads to difficult decisions and compromises. Some centers may be compelled to limit admissions or prioritize outpatient care over inpatient treatment to manage costs effectively. This practice, while cost-effective, may limit access to comprehensive care for individuals in need of intensive treatment.

Financial challenges also extend beyond operational costs to encompass the broader issue of societal attitudes toward addiction treatment. Stigma and discrimination persist, hindering efforts to raise awareness and garner support for addiction treatment initiatives. This societal reluctance to acknowledge addiction as a legitimate health concern further complicates fundraising efforts and resource allocation for addiction treatment centers.

Despite these formidable obstacles, addiction treatment professionals remain dedicated to their work. The impact of their efforts on the lives of countless individuals serves as a powerful source of motivation and inspiration. The opportunity to effect positive change in the lives of those struggling with addiction fuels their passion for their mission.

The inherent challenges of addiction treatment serve as a catalyst for innovation and growth within the field. Overcoming adversity fosters a spirit of willpower to overcome obstacles as well as achieve success. Addiction treatment professionals view these challenges as opportunities for learning and improvement, driving them to continually strive for excellence in their practice.

Financial adversities pose significant challenges to addiction treatment centers, yet they remain steadfast in their way, providing essential services to individuals struggling with addiction. Despite the ongoing obstacles, addiction treatment professionals draw strength and inspiration from their impact on the lives of those they serve. Their dedication exemplifies the transformative power of compassion, perseverance, and hope in the fight against addiction.

Establishing and maintaining a de-addiction center comes with numerous challenges, both expected and unexpected. From financial constraints to bureaucratic hurdles and societal stigmas, navigating these obstacles requires resilience. As someone deeply involved in the field of addiction treatment, Dr. Rajinder Singh has encountered various challenges throughout his career, but each presents unique opportunities for growth and advocacy.

He faced a considerable obstacle when establishing a de-addiction center in Jharon (Sangrur), where the Punjab government allotted to open a liquor vendor right in front of the facility. This decision posed a significant challenge, as patients passing by were frequently tempted to indulge in alcohol consumption, jeopardizing their progress in addiction treatment.

To mitigate this issue, Dr. Rajinder Singh implemented several measures. He began by writing letters to various governmental authorities, including the Chief Minister, Health Minister, and Ministry of Social Welfare, urging them to intervene. Despite multiple reminders and attempts to escalate the matter through legal channels, there was little response from the authorities. Dr. Rajinder Singh even contemplated filing a Public Interest Litigation (PIL), but the high costs associated with legal representation proved to be a significant barrier. Despite these challenges, he remained committed to finding a solution to the problem, recognizing the importance of creating a conducive environment for addiction recovery.

He refused to give up and decided to reach out to a judge whom he believed could help address the issue. To his surprise and relief, the judge took swift action, initiating a case against the Punjab government on his behalf. Legal proceedings ensued, and after numerous hearings, the judgment was finally delivered. The liquor vendor was ordered to be relocated 500 meters away from the center, a significant victory in their fight against addiction. Despite this success, the challenges persisted, with patients still being exposed to the temptation of alcohol consumption on their way to the center. Dr. Rajinder Singh continued to advocate for their well-being, submitting a revised petition to the judge requesting further action to ensure the complete removal of the liquor vendor from the vicinity of their facility.

The legal battle was arduous and time-consuming, spanning more than a year. Dr. Rajinder Singh had to navigate bureaucratic hurdles, meet with government officials, and persistently follow up on the progress of the case. Despite encountering resistance and delays, he remained steadfast in his constancy to safeguard the welfare of the patients. Ultimately, the liquor vendor was shifted to a far-off place.

In addition to the liquor vendor issue, Dr. Rajinder Singh faced another challenge when a former ward attendant opened an illegal de-addiction center in close proximity to theirs. This posed a potential threat to their reputation and credibility, as patients could easily be misled by the proximity of the competing facility and subjected to substandard treatment.

Despite these setbacks, he remained determined to overcome the obstacles and uphold the integrity of his de-addiction center and patients' well-being. Through perseverance, advocacy, and collaboration with legal authorities, he was able to overcome these challenges and continue his mission of providing comprehensive addiction treatment to those in need.

The experience taught him valuable lessons about purpose and the power of advocacy in effecting positive change. It reinforced his belief in the importance of standing up for what was right, even in the face of adversity. As a healthcare professional, it was his responsibility to advocate for the well-being of his patients and to ensure that they had access to the resources and support they needed to overcome addiction and lead fulfilling lives.

Looking back on those challenging times, he is proud of what they were able to accomplish and grateful for the support of the judiciary in addressing the issue of the liquor vendor. However, Dr. Rajinder Singh also recognizes that the fight against addiction is an ongoing battle that requires continued effort and vigilance.

As they move forward, he is committed to building on the progress they have made and finding new ways to support individuals struggling with addiction. Whether it is through expanding access to treatment services, raising awareness about the dangers of substance abuse, or advocating for policy changes, Dr. Rajinder Singh is dedicated to making a difference in the lives of those affected by addiction.

While overcoming the challenges associated with establishing and maintaining a de-addiction center has been difficult, it was also incredibly rewarding. The experiences and the lessons have shaped him into a stronger advocate for addiction treatment and recovery. With perseverance, he is confident that he can continue to make a positive impact through his fight against addiction.

Dr. Rajinder Singh's hard work in establishing and managing his de-addiction center was fraught with challenges, particularly in dealing with illegal competitors and political interference. One significant hurdle arose in the city center, where a rival facility, allegedly supported by politicians, posed a formidable threat. Patients seeking admission were often directed to this fake center, enticed by false promises regarding its treatment effectiveness.

Despite his diligent efforts to address the issue through legal channels and by seeking intervention from government authorities, progress remained elusive. Correspondence to high-ranking officials, including the Chief Minister, Health Minister, and Ministry of Social Welfare, failed to yield any response. Even meetings with top officials, such as the Principal Health Secretary, did not result in tangible action against the unlawful center.

The continued operation of the illegal establishment not only tarnished the reputation of Dr. Singh's facility but also undermined efforts to effectively combat addiction. Patients were being misled and diverted from receiving proper treatment, exacerbating the challenges in addressing addiction in the region. Despite repeated pleas for intervention, political influence and corruption appeared to impede meaningful action.

An important moment occurred when the Deputy Commissioner of Sangrur District took decisive action and raided the illegal center. Despite that and the subsequent arrest of the individual operating the center, political pressure hindered further steps. The involvement of politicians and officials in the drug trade highlighted the systemic challenges and corruption, hindering his efforts.

Beyond immediate challenges posed by illegal competitors, Dr. Rajinder Singh grappled with broader societal and political factors that fueled the drug trade. The immense profits generated by the drug industry, particularly in substances like heroin, incentivized corruption and criminal activity stared at him, yet he was helpless. Politicians and officials often played a role in this trade, complicating efforts to comprehensively address addiction.

Dr. Rajinder Singh's experiences highlighted the multifaceted nature of addressing addiction as a medical, social, psychological, and political issue. Despite his duty to provide comprehensive treatment and support to patients, systemic challenges and entrenched interests remained formidable. The fight against addiction demanded not only medical expertise but also advocacy, legal action, and political pressure for meaningful change.

Despite setbacks, he remained resolute in his devotion to patients and their well-being. His persistence in combating addiction and advocating for affected individuals demonstrated his resilience. As he navigated the complexities of his profession, Dr. Singh maintained hope that progress could one day be achieved in the fight against addiction.

In addition to confronting illegal competitors and political interference, Dr. Rajinder Singh faced logistical and financial obstacles in operating his de-addiction center. Limited resources and funding constraints posed significant challenges in providing comprehensive treatment and support to patients. Moreover, the high cost of maintaining a qualified medical team, particularly psychiatrists, strained the center's budget and hindered its ability to expand services.

The financial strain was exacerbated by the need to provide concessions and free services to accommodate the rural population, many of whom could not afford treatment. He recognized the importance of rendering maximum assistance to those in need, regardless of their financial circumstances, but acknowledged the difficulty in sustaining such efforts without adequate support.

However, Dr. Rajinder Singh remained committed to his mission of combating addiction and improving mental health outcomes in the community. Through strategic partnerships, fundraising efforts, and advocacy for increased government support, Dr. Rajinder Singh worked tirelessly to ensure that his center continued to serve those affected by addiction.

In addition to financial challenges, Dr. Rajinder Singh also navigated the complex dynamics of addiction treatment and recovery. He recognized the importance of addressing not only the physical aspects of addiction but also the underlying psychological and social factors contributing to substance abuse. Through holistic approaches that encompassed medical treatment, counseling, spiritual guidance, and community support, he sought to empower patients to overcome addiction and lead fulfilling lives.

His experiences with patients further deepened his understanding of addiction and its impact on individuals and families. He observed firsthand the devastating consequences of substance abuse, as well as the courage exhibited by those striving for recovery. These encounters reinforced his commitment to providing compassionate, evidence-based care and fueled his resolve to advocate for policies and initiatives that prioritize mental health and addiction treatment.

Despite the numerous challenges he faced, Dr. Rajinder Singh remained steadfast in his belief that addiction was a treatable condition and that every individual deserved access to quality care and support. His allegiance to his patients and his community served as an encouragement of hope in the fight against addiction, inspiring others to join him in the quest for a healthier, drug-free society.

Chapter 5

Thank You, Brother

Dr. Rajinder Singh reflects on the wholehearted influence that his brother, Gurbaksh Singh, had on his life. Gurbaksh, an advocate by profession, served not only as a guide but also as a trusted friend during pivotal moments. Despite their family's modest means, Gurbaksh's firm purpose propelled Dr. Singh toward a path that many deemed unattainable.

In the face of societal expectations and financial constraints, Gurbaksh fervently advocated for his brother's admission to a medical college. Despite the prevailing belief that such institutions were reserved for the elite, Gurbaksh refused to accept these limitations. With relentless strength of character, he rallied other family members, convincing them to support Dr. Rajinder Singh's aspirations.

Even in the face of skepticism from relatives, such as their uncle, Sardar Harbans Singh, Gurbaksh remained resolute. Sardar Harbans Singh's proverbial warnings only fueled Gurbaksh's willpower further. His commitment to his dreams was firm.

Through Gurbaksh's tireless efforts, Dr. Rajinder Singh secured admission to FSc (medical) at Government College Ludhiana after completing his matriculation. Despite the challenges ahead,

Gurbaksh's steadfast support and firm belief in Dr. Singh's potential served as a ray of hope during moments of doubt.

In spite of his brother's reassuring words and encouragement, Dr. Singh found himself grappling with numerous challenges. Financial constraints weighed heavily on him, casting a shadow over his dreams of pursuing a medical education.

As a day scholar, he faced the arduous task of commuting daily from his aunt's home in Sultanwind Gate, Amritsar, to the medical college on foot, a trip spanning six to seven kilometers on each side. The relentless cycle of early mornings, classes, and late evenings at the hospital took a toll on him, contrasting sharply with the comfort of studying at home in Ludhiana.

The transition from the familiar surroundings of home to the demands of medical college proved to be a daunting task for Dr. Rajinder Singh. Despite his brother's uplifting words, the reality of his circumstances posed significant obstacles in his strive toward his aspirations.

Despite the immense difficulties, he found solace and strength in his brother's inspiring letters. There were moments when he contemplated giving up, yet his brother's words of encouragement spurred him to persevere.

Ultimately, Dr. Rajinder Singh's persistence paid off, leading him to success. Reflecting on his journey, he recalls a powerful analogy shared by his uncle, who worked in a locomotive shed. His uncle drew parallels between the workings of an engine and a man and his pursuits. An engine requires fuel, and man requires food and water. None can function without the required fuel. To thrive, his brother emphasized the importance of fueling one's aspirations with tenacity and effort.

Much like stoking a fire to generate steam and power an engine, Dr. Singh's brother urged him to engage with his studies and interact with professors, emphasizing the transformative power of education. His brother's firm support, guidance, and mentorship revolutionized Dr. Rajinder Singh's life.

Despite the financial strain on his family, his brother remained a steadfast source of encouragement. Even though their circumstances made it challenging for him to provide financial support, his brother's firm belief in Dr. Singh's abilities never wavered.

Despite facing skepticism from others, including his family, Dr. Singh's brother continued to uplift him with words of encouragement, albeit with a hint of playful teasing. He acknowledged the difficulties they faced but never allowed him to lose sight of his dreams.

Dr. Singh recalls his brother's analogy of the engine, highlighting the distinction between mechanical operations and human motivation. While others may have dismissed his brother's words, he held onto them, finding strength in his firm support.

In the end, Dr. Singh's persistence paid off, and he achieved his dream of becoming a doctor. His brother, despite not being able to offer financial assistance, was overjoyed at his success. Dr. Singh acknowledges that the true measure of support lies not in monetary contributions but in the firm encouragement and positive attitude his brother provided, serving as an invaluable source of inspiration.

He reminisces about the fluctuating emotions he experienced while reading his brother's letters. At times, he would feel determined to persevere, spurred on by his brother's firm encouragement. However, there were moments of doubt when he questioned his path, considering the possibility of settling for a simpler career as a clerk after completing his FSc.

Despite his wavering resolve, Dr. Rajinder Singh's brother remained a constant source of support, continuing to send him uplifting letters. These missives served as a lifeline, reaffirming his responsibility to his education and providing him with the strength to overcome his doubts.

Ultimately, Dr. Singh completed his graduation, thanks in no small part to his brother's persistent encouragement. Even beyond this milestone, his brother's idealistic outlook on the world and society continued to influence him, shaping his own views within the family and beyond.

Dr. Singh reflects on the cultural norms of the 1920s and 1930s, particularly highlighting the common practice of *ghungat,* which was prevalent among women during that era. However, his elder brother's disapproval of such customs made him salute his brother's thoughts. Despite being highly educated and knowledgeable, his brother struggled financially, but his wisdom left a lasting impression on the younger brother.

Additionally, Dr. Rajinder Singh acknowledges the simplicity and devotion of his parents, who, although they did not explicitly preach to him, provided a powerful example through their way of life. Their humility served as a guiding light for him, shaping his values and beliefs in powerful ways.

Dr. Singh reminisces about his brother's love for reading and writing, despite all the challenges. He fondly recalls his sister-in-law's humorous remark, comparing his brother to Mirza Ghalib and Karl Marx.

His brother was deeply interested in the works of notable figures like Karl Marx, Immanuel Kant, and Abraham Lincoln, often citing their perseverance in learning despite adverse circumstances. Dr. Singh drew inspiration from his brother's encouragement, reflecting on the idea that if others can overcome obstacles and achieve greatness, so can he. This steadfast belief in the power of resolution continues to motivate him in his endeavors to date.

Dr. Rajinder Singh fondly remembers the influential role his family played in shaping his character, noting that they taught him through their actions rather than words. Their exemplary behavior served as a powerful form of guidance, instilling in him values of simplicity, devotion, and hard work.

In addition to his family, Dr. Singh found support and inspiration among his friends during his time at the medical college and the Government College in Ludhiana. His friends, who shared his passion for learning, were not only helpful but also served as motivation for him to excel academically.

He recalls with pride the achievements of his friends, including one who went on to become an engineer and was among the first to secure admission to IIT Kharagpur from their Government College in Ludhiana. Their success further fueled his own determination to pursue excellence in his academic endeavors.

Dr. Singh also recalls the camaraderie he shared with his friends during his time at the medical college. Despite the physical distance that separated them as some pursued different paths, their bond remained strong.

Reflecting on his days at the medical college, Dr. Singh recalls the enjoyment they found in their studies, tempered by moments of regret over the challenges they faced. Yet, even in the midst of hardship, he found solace in the words of his brother, which lent him a sense of perspective.

Dr. Rajinder Singh vividly remembers the early morning rush to reach class on time, a daily trek of several kilometers. Despite his best efforts, he often found himself arriving late, an attestation to the physical and logistical hurdles he faced as a student. Yet, even in these tough moments, Dr. Singh drew strength from the shared experiences and support of his friends.

Dr. Singh fondly recollects his days in the medical college, where his casual attire, particularly his preference for colorful pajamas, set him apart from his peers. While others wore traditional trousers, he opted for the comfort of pajamas, albeit in vibrant hues, more commonly seen in nightwear.

His unconventional choice caught the attention of their physical instructor, who advised him to switch to a more standard attire of white pajamas and shirts. Dr. Rajinder Singh complied, recognizing the importance of conforming to expectations in certain situations.

Amidst the academic rigors, his wife emerged as a light of inspiration and support. Despite facing initial hurdles during their marriage, their loyalty to each other helped them weather the storms, ultimately strengthening their bond. Dr. Rajinder Singh credits his wife for her firm devotion and guidance, which played a pivotal role in shaping his whole life and career.

Dr. Singh reflects on the invaluable support he received from his wife, who was not only his colleague but also his senior in medical college. Despite the age gap, their relationship blossomed, with his wife providing crucial assistance during his pursuit of post-graduation.

Dr. Rajinder Singh obtained his DPM degree from Pune, with his wife's firm cooperation playing a pivotal role. Despite juggling familial responsibilities, including caring for their two children, Neelam and their younger child, his wife passionately supported Dr. Rajinder in his academic endeavors.

While Dr. Singh describes himself as reserved and shy compared to his outgoing wife, he appreciates her sociable nature and zest for life. Her enthusiasm for socializing, attending parties, and going on outings contrasts with his more introverted demeanor.

Despite their initial differences and staying apart for a long time due to postings, Dr. Singh acknowledges his wife's proactive approach to enriching their lives through travel and exploration. It was her initiative that led them to visit various destinations like Kashmir, Dalhousie, Shimla, and various other places, creating cherished memories for their family.

Moving on, Dr. Rajinder Singh briefly mentions a patient he encountered during his tenure as a Senior Advisor in Psychiatry in Calcutta. As part of his responsibilities, he oversaw the final disposition of the officer patient referred to his department. This anecdote provides insight into Dr. Singh's professional experience and the diverse challenges he encountered in his career.

Dr. Singh recalls a significant case involving a Major in the army referred to him for psychiatric evaluation. Despite no apparent psychiatric abnormalities, the Major struggled with difficulties in his military duties. As a member of the Army Supply Corps (ASC) tasked with providing essential provisions such as milk and food to the troops, his role was critical for the well-being of his fellow soldiers.

During their consultation, the Major disclosed distressing experiences of harassment and intimidation from his senior officers. These incidents stemmed from his attempts to address underlying issues within the army, highlighting the challenges faced by those who advocate for change within hierarchical structures. Despite his noble intentions, the Major found himself targeted and threatened for speaking out against injustices.

The intensity of the Major's distress was unmistakable, underscoring the emotional toll of confronting systemic problems in professional environments. This case serves as a poignant reminder of the complexities surrounding mental health in such settings, where power struggles and organizational dynamics can exacerbate psychological struggles.

Dr. Singh recounts the treatment of the Major, who had developed depression as a reaction to the harassment he had faced from his senior officers. Despite undergoing various treatments, including electroconvulsive therapy (ECT), the Major's depression persisted.

After observing that the Major's condition did not improve over a period of more than two months, Dr. Rajinder Singh made the difficult decision to recommend his invalidation from the army. This recommendation was based on the Major's inability to function effectively within the military due to his depression and the ongoing harassment he endured.

Dr. Singh's decision to recommend invalidation diverged from the viewpoint of the referring psychiatrist, who believed the Major was an administrative problem causing disruptions within the unit. This decision brings out Dr. Rajinder Singh's will to prioritize the well-being of his patients, even in the face of differing opinions and bureaucratic pressures. It highlights the complexities involved in navigating mental health issues within professional settings, particularly in the army, where administrative and disciplinary considerations often intersect with medical care.

Dr. Singh recounts a challenging situation he faced after giving his final opinion on the case of the Major in Delhi. Despite recommending the Major's invalidation from the army due to his ongoing depression and harassment, rumors began circulating that Dr. Singh had accepted a large sum of money to facilitate the Major's invalidation.

The rumors reached the higher echelons of the army, leading to Dr. Singh being summoned by the Director of Medical Services in the Army (DMS). Despite pressure to reconsider his opinion, he stood by his decision, asserting that he had given the matter thorough consideration and believed his opinion to be correct.

Ultimately, the Major was invalidated from the army, and Dr. Rajinder Singh's steadfastness in his decision was vindicated. However, the rumors persisted, with some questioning his integrity and insinuating that he had accepted bribes.

Despite the challenges and accusations he faced, he remained resolute in his word to uphold what he believed was right. His firm devotion to his principles and his patients' well-being prevailed, demonstrating his integrity and ethical conduct in the face of adversity.

Dr. Singh also reflects on the hierarchical culture of the army, where obedience to superior officers is paramount, regardless of the circumstances. Despite this, he remained steadfast in his decision-making process, guided by his ethical principles and commitment to his patients' well-being.

Following his retirement from the army, Dr. Rajinder Singh transitioned to working at a de-addiction center, where he encountered several notable cases involving addiction to substances like heroin and alcohol. These experiences further deepened his understanding of mental health and addiction treatment.

Overall, these experiences emphasized Dr. Singh's duty to psychiatry and his willingness to confront challenges and advocate for what he believes is right, even in environments where questioning authority may be frowned upon.

Dr. Singh reflects on the evolution of psychiatry as a medical specialty, noting its previous stigma and the subsequent fillip in prestige. In contemporary times, psychiatry is recognized as a highly valued branch of medicine, with practitioners commanding substantial salaries, especially in the face of rising addiction rates and associated complexities.

He highlights the unique challenges of addiction treatment, including patient non-compliance, distorted priorities, stigma, and criminality. He highlights the global nature of the addiction crisis and the scarcity of psychiatrists trained to address it effectively.

Regarding his quest in psychiatry, Dr. Singh acknowledges the influence of mentors like Dr. Vidya Sagar, whose expertise inspired him to pursue specialization despite initial limitations. Through his military service, he was able to advance his qualifications in psychiatry, fulfilling his aspirations and contributing to the field. His journey underscores the importance of mentorship in achieving professional goals, ultimately benefiting both patients and the healthcare community at large.

Dr. Singh reminisces about his belief in serving with perseverance, pledging to return twice the service he received. He was to the structured environment and lack of political interference within the army, preferring it over the civil service.

Throughout his military career, he enjoyed the numerous facilities provided by the army, including exceptional medical care even after retirement. He reflects fondly on his time in the army, considering it a blessing that enriched his life in many ways.

Dr. Singh recalls many colleagues and friends from his time in the army, and Brigadier (Dr.) Jagjit Singh Bhalla is one among them. They were classmates during their BSc studies at the Government College in Ludhiana. His friendship with Dr. Bhalla endured, reflecting the strength of their bond and the shared experiences that forged their connection. Their bond continued as they pursued their medical education and later served together in the army.

Dr. Rajinder Singh also mentions another close colleague, Air Commodore Dr. Surjit Singh, with whom he shared experiences both in medical college and in their military service. Their camaraderie remains strong as they continue to meet frequently even in their post-retirement years.

He reflects on a recent get-together with other medical college classmates, highlighting the enduring friendships forged during their shared experiences through education and military service. These connections serve as a demonstration of the lasting bonds formed through shared experiences and mutual support.

Dr. Singh reflects on a memorable patient from his time in the army, noting that while there were many patients, one stands out as particularly special. He acknowledges that alcoholism was prevalent among military personnel, often exacerbated by the easy availability and affordability of alcohol, especially in high-altitude areas where it was included as part of rations.

Despite this cultural norm, Dr. Singh emphasizes his belief that alcohol is not a solution for relieving stress or tension. According to him, this issue is not unique to the Indian Army but a global phenomenon influenced by broader social norms and practices.

Dr. Rajinder Singh's awareness of the challenges posed by alcoholism among military personnel underlined his duty to address mental health issues within the army and advocate for more effective as well as holistic approaches to promoting well-being among service members.

Dr. Singh shares his personal perspective on relaxation and the use of alcohol. He believes that while many people around the world gather to drink and unwind, there are more constructive and positive ways to relax, such as music, meditation, jogging, and immersing oneself in nature.

He highlights that these activities offer genuine and long-lasting relaxation, unlike the temporary relief provided by alcohol, which, according to him, is a negative form of relaxation due to its addictive nature and potential for lifelong problems. He holds the belief that alcoholism has caused significant harm globally, making it a major contributor to various social and health issues.

He concludes by acknowledging that while his viewpoint may not be universally shared, it is essential for him to prioritize healthier and more sustainable approaches to relaxation and stress relief.

Dr. Singh discusses his work in the field of addiction treatment following his retirement, highlighting the devastating impact of alcohol on individuals, families, and society as a whole. He underscores the importance of education and awareness in preventing substance abuse, particularly among young people.

To address this need for awareness, Dr. Rajinder Singh and his colleagues have authored a book titled 'Be Aware and Be Aware of Drugs', which is distributed during workshops and to students. He stresses that prevention through education is paramount, as once individuals become addicted, overcoming substance abuse becomes a difficult, costly, and long-lasting problem.

Dr. Singh highlights the difficulty of treating addiction due to the changes it causes to the brain, coupled with the scarcity and expense of mental health professionals. He characterizes addiction as a chronic and relapsing illness, highlighting the need for ongoing support and resources for those struggling with substance abuse.

He expresses his belief in the importance of prevention through education and awareness regarding the hazards of substance abuse. He believes that educating individuals about the risks associated with addiction is crucial in mitigating its impact on individuals and society.

In addition to discussing addiction prevention, Dr. Rajinder Singh also shares his admiration for Sant Baba Iqbal Singh Ji's dedicated service to humanity. He recounts his experiences visiting Baru Sahib for medical camps, where he and his wife provided free medical services.

Dr. Rajinder Singh reflects on the passage of starting his efforts in addiction treatment, recalling how Sant Baba Iqbal Singh Ji's encouragement prompted him to initiate the endeavor. Initially working alone, he gradually gathered a team of dedicated professionals, including a psychologist, a psychiatrist from America, a medical officer from Japan, and a psychiatrist from Bombay.

Chapter 6

The Kalgidhar Trust: Fostering Hope

At Baru Sahib, a divine valley nestled in the serene landscapes of Himachal Pradesh, a light of hope shines amidst the shadows of drug addiction. The Kalgidhar Trust, a globally recognized humanitarian organization founded by Sant Baba Iqbal Singh Ji, has emerged as a leading force in the battle against this pervasive malady, particularly rampant among the youth in Punjab and its neighboring regions.

The scourge of drug addiction is a complex issue that not only ravages individuals but also corrodes the fabric of societies. In Punjab, once celebrated for its rich culture and industrious people, the grip of addiction has left a trail of despair and shattered dreams. Recognizing the urgent need for intervention, on the directions of Sant Baba Iqbal Singh Ji, Dr. Rajinder through The Kalgidhar Trust, embarked on a mission to offer more than just conventional treatments.

The Kalgidhar Trust is dedicated to addressing the pressing issue of drug addiction, which plagues society at large particularly the youth of Punjab and neighboring regions. In response to this pervasive challenge, the Trust has pioneered an innovative approach that combines modern medical interventions with the transformative practices of yoga and spiritual therapy. This unique blend aims to enhance the recovery process and has led to the establishment of two Akal Drug De-Addiction and Rehabilitation Centres, strategically located in Punjab and Himachal Pradesh, at Cheema Sahib and Baru Sahib, respectively.

These centers serve as sanctuaries of healing, providing a holistic approach to recovery that addresses not only the physical dependence on addiction but also the psychological and spiritual dimensions of addiction.

Central to the success of The Kalgidhar Trust's approach is the integration of modern medical techniques with age-old practices of yoga and spiritual practice. By combining evidence-based medical treatments with yoga 'asanas', pranayama, and meditation, individuals are empowered to reclaim control over their bodies and minds. Yoga, with its emphasis on holistic well-being, serves as a powerful tool in alleviating stress, anxiety, and depression—the common triggers for substance abuse.

Moreover, spiritual practice plays an important role in reconnecting individuals with their inner selves and fostering a sense of purpose and belonging. Through counseling, mindfulness practices, and participation in community rituals, addicts are guided on a path of self-actualization and evolution. This spiritual dimension not only instills hope but also cultivates resilience, equipping individuals with the strength to navigate life's challenges without resorting to substance abuse.

Beyond the treatment of addiction, The Kalgidhar Trust is committed to addressing the root cause of the problem through prevention and education initiatives. Awareness campaigns, workshops, and outreach programs are conducted to educate communities about the dangers of drug abuse and promote healthy lifestyles. By fostering a culture of prevention and early intervention, the Trust aims to stem the tide of addiction before it takes root.

The impact of Dr. Singh's efforts extends far beyond the walls of the rehabilitation centers. By empowering individuals to break free from the shackles of addiction, he is sowing the seeds of a shift within families and communities. Restoring dignity and hope to those once trapped in the grip of despair, he is paving the way for a brighter future for generations to come.

In addition to its work in addiction rehabilitation, The Kalgidhar Trust is engaged in a myriad of humanitarian initiatives aimed at uplifting the marginalized and vulnerable sections of society. From providing education and healthcare to empowering women and promoting sustainable agriculture, the Trust's holistic approach to social welfare embodies the spirit of *seva* (selfless service) and compassion.

As we reflect on the impact of Kalgidhar Trust's endeavors, we are reminded of the enduring power of human kindness and resilience. In the face of seemingly insurmountable challenges, it is the resolve of individuals and organizations like The Kalgidhar Trust that restores faith in the inherent goodness of humanity.

As the sun sets on another day in Punjab and Himachal Pradesh, the light of hope continues to shine brightly, illuminating the path to recovery and renewal. Dr. Rajinder Singh through Kalgidhar Trust is not only transforming lives but also inspiring a movement of compassion and solidarity that knows no bounds.

At Baru Sahib, a quiet revolution is underway—a mission fueled by compassion and driven by a vision of reformation. The Kalgidhar Trust, a hope for countless souls, has embarked upon a noble endeavor to combat the scourge of drug addiction that plagues rural communities, particularly among those who struggle to access quality healthcare.

Recognizing the impact of drug addiction on individuals, families, and society at large, The Kalgidhar Trust has launched its health mission, aptly titled 'Envisaging a Drug-Free Society'. At its core lies a guarantee to provide holistic treatment to rural, low-income individuals who often find themselves trapped in the vicious cycle of addiction, devoid of adequate resources and support.

Under the divine guidance of Padma Shri, Shiromani Panth Rattan, Late Baba Iqbal Singh Ji, the Trust conceived a bold vision: to establish Akal Drug De-Addiction and Rehabilitation Centres across Punjab—sanctuaries of healing where individuals could find solace, support, and the tools for evolution. The two existing centers, managed by a dedicated team of seasoned experts, offer more than just medical treatment; they provide a holistic approach that integrates medicine, yoga, and spiritual practice.

In rural communities where access to quality healthcare is often limited, the establishment of these centers represents a light of hope. Here, individuals from all walks of life, irrespective of their socio-economic status, find refuge and renewal. The resolve toward recovery begins with a comprehensive assessment by highly experienced professionals who tailor treatment plans to meet the unique needs of each individual.

Moreover, spiritual therapy plays a pivotal role in guiding individuals on a voyage of self-searching. Rooted in the rich spiritual heritage of the region, this aspect of the treatment process fosters a sense of purpose, meaning, and connection to something greater than oneself. Through counseling, mindfulness practices, and participation in community rituals, individuals are empowered to heal not only their bodies but also their souls.

Beyond the confines of the rehabilitation centers, The Kalgidhar Trust's health mission extends its reach through a variety of outreach programs and initiatives. Community awareness campaigns, educational workshops, and preventive interventions are conducted to address the root causes of addiction and promote healthy lifestyles. By engaging with local communities and fostering collaboration with government agencies and NGOs, the Trust seeks to create a supportive ecosystem that empowers individuals to lead fulfilling, drug-free lives.

As the sun rises over the verdant fields of Punjab and the mist-clad hills of Himachal Pradesh, the light of hope shines ever brighter. Through its tireless efforts, The Kalgidhar Trust is not merely treating addiction; it is sowing the seeds of shift and renewal within rural communities. Each success story is an indication of the resilience of the human spirit and the power of compassion to overcome even the most formidable challenges.

The Kalgidhar Trust's health mission stands as a shining thread—a symbol of hope, healing, and humanity. As it continues to build ahead on its expedition toward a drug-free society, it invites us all to join hands in solidarity, compassion, and service to those in need. Together, we can build a brighter future, one where every individual has the opportunity to thrive, flourish, and fulfill their highest potential.

In the calm countryside of Sangrur district, Punjab, amidst the lush fields and serene surroundings, lies a sanctuary of hope and healing—the Akal Drug De-Addiction and Rehabilitation Centre at Cheema Sahib. Established in 2004 by The Kalgidhar Trust, this center stands as a lighthouse of hope in the battle against drug addiction, offering a lifeline to those grappling with the scourge of substance abuse.

The solid endeavor to establish the Akal Drug De-Addiction and Rehabilitation Centre began with a deep concern for the escalating drug problem, particularly among the youth. Padma Shri, Late Baba Iqbal Singh Ji, a revered spiritual leader, recognized the urgent need for action and exhorted Dr. Rajinder to spearhead efforts to tackle this menace.

With the blessing and guidance of Baba Ji, Dr. Rajinder embarked on a long and arduous ride, driven by a firm resolve to bring back the youth gone astray and restore hope in their lives. Thus, the foundation was laid for the establishment of the Akal Drug De-Addiction and Rehabilitation Centre—a confirmation of the resolute belief of The Kalgidhar Trust to serve the community and alleviate human suffering.

Since its inception, the Akal Drug De-Addiction and Rehabilitation Centre at Cheema Sahib has emerged as the largest center in rural Punjab, boasting 30 beds dedicated to the treatment and rehabilitation of individuals battling addiction. What sets this center apart is not just its size but its outstanding success rate—a commendable 60 percent abstinence rate, surpassing global standards. This achievement is evidence of the effectiveness of the holistic approach employed by the center, which integrates modern medicine, yoga, and spiritual practice.

At the heart of the center's success is its highly experienced team of experts, comprising medical professionals, yoga instructors, and spiritual counselors. Together, they collaborate to provide personalized care and support to each individual, addressing not only the physical dependence on drugs but also the underlying psychological and spiritual aspects of addiction.

The treatment at the Akal Drug De-Addiction and Rehabilitation Centre begins with a comprehensive assessment, followed by a tailored treatment plan designed to meet the unique needs of each patient. Medical interventions, including detoxification and medication-assisted therapy, are complemented by holistic practices such as yoga 'asanas', breathing exercises, and meditation. These practices not only promote physical well-being but also foster inner peace, resilience, and self-awareness, which are essential qualities for long-term recovery.

Moreover, spiritual practice as part of treatment plays a crucial role in guiding individuals on a cruise of introspection. Through counseling, mindfulness practices, and participation in spiritual quests, patients are empowered to reconnect with their inner selves and find meaning and purpose in life beyond addiction.

As the sun rises over the tranquil fields of Cheema Sahib, a new day dawns—one filled with hope, healing, and the promise of renewal. Through the tireless efforts of The Kalgidhar Trust and its esteemed team of professionals, the Akal Drug De-Addiction and Rehabilitation Centre continues to be a light for those in need, offering a path to recovery and a chance at a brighter future.

Nestled in the picturesque landscapes of the Sirmour district in Himachal Pradesh is a sanctuary of healing and renewal—the Akal Drug De-Addiction and Rehabilitation Centre at Baru Sahib. Established in July 2016 by The Kalgidhar Trust, this center helps individuals grappling with the debilitating effects of drug addiction. Situated amidst the divine valley at the village of Baru Sahib, this center offers not only medical treatment but also the healing power of nature, spiritual resonance, and holistic care.

The decision to establish the Akal Drug De-Addiction and Rehabilitation Centre at Baru Sahib was proof of The Kalgidhar Trust's commitment to expanding its reach and addressing the pressing needs of rural communities. Serving as the Trust's second center, it brought much-needed relief to individuals in Himachal Pradesh and neighboring areas who were battling addiction without adequate support or resources.

One of the unique features of the Akal Drug De-Addiction and Rehabilitation Centre at Baru Sahib is its status as the only private center in Himachal Pradesh offering inpatient facilities for women. This important addition acknowledges the diverse needs of individuals struggling with addiction and ensures that women have access to specialized care as well as support tailored to their unique circumstances.

The center, boasting 50 beds and both outpatient and inpatient facilities, is situated within the premises of the Akal Charitable Hospital, Baru Sahib—a 100-bed general hospital. This strategic location ensures seamless access to a range of medical services and diagnostic facilities, further enhancing the quality of care provided to patients seeking treatment for addiction.

Beyond its functional amenities, what truly sets the Akal Drug De-Addiction and Rehabilitation Centre apart is its serene setting. Surrounded by the majestic mountains of Himachal Pradesh and enveloped in the spiritual resonance of Gurdwara Sahib, the center offers a healing environment conducive to recovery and introspection. Patients have the opportunity to reconnect with nature, breathe clean air, and find solace amidst the beauty of their surroundings, which is a therapeutic experience in itself.

The holistic approach adopted by the center encompasses not only medical treatment but also the integration of yoga and spiritual practice into the recovery process. Patients are guided through a comprehensive treatment regimen that addresses the physical, psychological, and spiritual dimensions of addiction, ensuring a well-rounded approach to healing.

Under the compassionate care of a dedicated team of professionals, including medical practitioners, yoga instructors, and spiritual counselors, patients embark on a process of self-introspection. Through a combination of evidence-based medical interventions, yoga 'asanas', breathing exercises, and meditation, individuals learn to cultivate inner strength, resilience, and self-awareness—essential qualities for long-term recovery.

Spiritual therapy plays a significant role in guiding patients toward inner peace and harmony. Through counseling, mindfulness practices, and participation in spiritual practices, individuals are empowered to reconnect with their inner selves and rediscover a sense of purpose and meaning in life beyond addiction.

As the sun sets over the valley of Baru Sahib, the Akal Drug De-Addiction and Rehabilitation Centre continues to serve as hope and healing for individuals seeking to break free from the shackles of addiction. Through its devotion to holistic care and its embrace of nature's healing power, the center offers a pathway to renewal and a brighter future for all those who walk through its doors.

Drug addiction is a complex and pervasive issue that goes beyond individual health concerns and affects families, communities, and societies at large. Particularly prevalent among male youth and adolescents, drug addiction not only wreaks havoc on physical and mental health but also disrupts familial and societal harmony. The adverse consequences extend beyond the individual, contributing to increased crime rates and societal instability. In essence, drug addiction erodes the very fabric of society, necessitating a comprehensive and concerted response.

Recognizing the multifaceted nature of drug addiction and its far-reaching impact, The Kalgidhar Trust, based in Baru Sahib, Himachal Pradesh, has undertaken a proactive stance in addressing this pressing issue. With a mission to tackle drug addiction wholeheartedly through medical, familial, societal, and spiritual quests, the Trust launched the Akal Drug De-Addiction campaign in 2004, setting the stage for a transformative sail toward healing and recovery.

The approach adopted by The Kalgidhar Trust's Drug De-Addiction Centres is holistic, encompassing a blend of traditional and spiritual components alongside medical interventions. With an emphasis on family therapy, group counseling, and engagement in indoor and outdoor activities, the treatment regimen is tailored to address the physical, psychological, and spiritual dimensions of addiction. This multidimensional approach reflects the Trust's devotion to addressing the root causes of addiction and promoting long-term recovery as well as wellness.

Central to the success of The Kalgidhar Trust's approach is the recognition of drug addiction as a preventable disability, morbidity, and a leading cause of death. By providing holistic treatment and support, the Trust aims to reduce the number of individuals suffering from drug dependence and empower them to lead fulfilling lives, free from the shackles of addiction. However, the trip toward recovery does not end with treatment; it requires ongoing support and follow-up, both from healthcare professionals and the patient's family.

Efforts to combat drug addiction must extend beyond the confines of treatment centers. The Trust emphasizes the importance of seeking family support and reducing the availability of drugs in communities. Additionally, initiatives to control illicit drug trafficking and raise awareness about drug abuse, particularly among vulnerable segments of society, are critical components of the overarching strategy.

Parents, teachers, and educators play an important role in prevention efforts, equipping individuals with the knowledge and skills to make informed choices and resist peer pressure. Moreover, the role of spiritualism in regulating individual, family, and social life cannot be overstated. Practices such as meditation, prayer, and engagement in spiritual quests have the potential to shape thoughts and judgments, offering a powerful deterrent against drug abuse and aiding in the rehabilitation of addicts.

In sum, The Kalgidhar Trust's holistic approach to combating drug addiction exemplifies the power of collective action and compassion in addressing one of society's most pressing challenges. Through its resolute dedication to holistic care, community engagement, and spiritual guidance, the Trust is paving the way for a brighter future—one where individuals can break free from the chains of addiction and reclaim their lives with dignity and purpose.

Drug addiction is a chronic and relapsing mental disorder affecting particularly male youth and adolescents. It not only causes adverse effects on the physical, mental, and moral health of the individual but the family life also gets grossly disturbed. The prevalence of drug abuse in society makes it unwholesome, and the rate of crime also increases. In fact, it erodes the very existence of society. To start with, a drug is taken for pleasure, but gradually with the development of tolerance and craving, it becomes a compulsion. Various socio-cultural factors have also been found to be significantly correlated with drug abuse. Religious or spiritual pursuits have a powerful influence on a person's psyche and life in Eastern culture.

Collectively, drug addiction is a leading cause of preventable disability, morbidity, and death. Addiction needs to be tackled wholeheartedly by medical, familial, societal, and spiritual means.

The Kalgidhar Trust is coming up with the third state-of-the-art drug de-addiction center at Chunni Kalan, Fatehgarh Sahib, in Punjab shortly. Dr. Rajinder Singh says they manage their patients through holistic treatment, comprising a blend of traditional and spiritual components with an emphasis on family therapy, group counseling, and engagement of patients in indoor and outdoor games. Fifty thousand-plus have benefited from the treatment at both centers so far.

The treatment has to be multidimensional, so efforts should be made to seek family support besides a reduction in the availability and demand for drugs. "Through treatment at these centers, we can reduce the number of persons suffering from drug dependence. It is important for the patients to visit the centers regularly for follow-ups, along with the family members. Poor follow-up is directly related to the poor outcome. It is, however, more important to make concerted efforts to control illicit drug trafficking, and to lay emphasis on education and creating awareness about drug abuse, especially among the vulnerable segment of society," says Dr. Rajinder Singh.

He opines that drug addiction has multiple causes and its management requires a multi-pronged approach. The role of parents, teachers, and educators cannot be overemphasized in preventing this menace. He believes spiritualism, which has the potential to regulate individual, family, and social life, plays a crucial role in minimizing and eradicating drugs from society. Meditation, prayer, and spiritual practices impact our thoughts and judgments and hence can be very useful in preventing drug abuse, as well as managing and rehabilitating drug addicts.

Chapter 7

Values for Life

Kirat Karo (earn your livelihood honestly)

Naam Japo (remember God; recite His name)

Vand Chhako (share your boons with the needy)

Dr. Rajinder Singh says it is the accumulation of values that is his treasure. "First of all, everyone has ethical, moral, and spiritual values. So, from the beginning, from his childhood, from his adolescence, from the time he came to his senses, from that time itself, he has been speaking the truth and serving people." He reflects on the significance of values, seeing them as the true treasure of human existence. Throughout his life, from childhood to adolescence and beyond, he has embraced ethical, moral, and spiritual principles as guiding lights. What strikes him most is the innate nature of these values; they were not learned but rather ingrained within him from the very beginning.

In reminiscing about his past, Dr. Rajinder Singh recalls a poignant incident from his youth. A simple trip to the pharmacy stands out vividly in his memory. As a school or college student, he went to purchase medicine and, to his surprise, received an extra paisa than expected. In an act that seemed almost instinctual, he promptly returned the excess amount to the pharmacist, despite his young age and the small sum involved. This act of honesty and integrity left a lasting impression on both Dr. Singh and the pharmacist, who warmly appreciated his gesture.

This anecdote serves as a powerful witness to Dr. Singh's solid vow to his values, even when faced with seemingly trivial choices. It deepens the essence of his character and the depth of his conviction in living a life governed by principles of truth and service to others.

In his family, his elder brother played a significant role as a guide and mentor. His brother was quite the revolutionary for his time, rejecting traditional customs, like the mandatory covering of their faces with veils, that constrained women. Back in the 1920s and 1930s, this was highly uncommon, but his brother stood firm in his beliefs.

Unlike the norm of the day, which emphasized finding a job after completing the 10th grade, Dr. Singh's brother placed great value on education. He believed in putting in the effort to excel academically and upheld the importance of a large, extended family living together, in contrast with the trend toward smaller, nuclear families today.

He acknowledges that he had inherited these values from his brother, cherishing the emphasis on education and the sense of community that his brother instilled in their family.

In Dr. Singh's family, the values of integrity, resilience, and devotion ran deep, passed down from generation to generation. His father, despite having only a third or fourth-grade education, possessed a profound reverence for Shri Guru Gobind Singh Ji, the 10th Sikh Guru. He wrote a book of poems titled 'Mera Sikhi Siddiq' out of sheer devotion, not for publication but as a personal expression of faith. His father's solid commitment to his beliefs was evident in his dedication to writing, despite his limited formal education. He found solace and purpose in sharing stories of Guru Gobind Singh's sacrifices and teachings, which instilled courage and inspiration in his children, including Dr. Rajinder Singh himself.

Life wasn't easy for the family. His mother faced postpartum psychiatric issues, adding to the challenges they already encountered. Living in a cramped single room in Lahore with a large family tested their resilience daily. Yet, his father confronted these adversities with courage and grace, never once complaining about their circumstances.

Despite financial hardships and the scarcity of resources, his father refused to compromise his principles. When his brother-in-law suggested that he remarry to alleviate their domestic woes, he completely declined, prioritizing loyalty and assurance to his family above all else. His refusal, imbued with integrity and steadfastness, left a lasting impression on him as a child.

In a society where it was common for people to abandon their partner in times of hardship, his father's resolute loyalty and sacrificial love for his lifemate and children stood out as a light of strength and honor. His refusal to abandon his wife, even in the face of dire circumstances, exemplified the values of loyalty and selflessness that Dr. Rajinder Singh deeply admired and internalized.

Dr. Singh's upbringing in such an environment sincerely shaped his own values and outlook on life. He learned the importance of standing firm in one's beliefs, even in the face of adversity, and the value of unconditional love and loyalty to the family.

Through his father's example, he gleaned invaluable lessons in resilience, integrity, and devotion, which continue to guide him in his own journey. His father's unwavering commitment to his principles and his family left an indelible mark on his character, inspiring him to lead a life rooted in integrity, compassion, and service to others.

In essence, his family legacy is one of strength, resilience, and devotion—a legacy that continues to shape and inspire him to this day.

Dr. Rajinder Singh's flight through life has been shaped by a rich painting of experiences, teachings, and values passed down through generations. Rooted in the religiosity of his family's values, his upbringing instilled in him a deep reverence for principles that guided his path.

His student days were characterized by simplicity and a reluctance to engage in social interactions, a trait uncommon among his peers. Despite the prevailing culture, he remained steadfast in his convictions, steering clear of the popularity-seeking behaviors often indulged in by others. This choice, however, came with its share of challenges. He endured struggles in both his academic pursuits and personal life, facing obstacles that tested his resolve.

Driven by a thirst for knowledge, he found solace in reading and reflection. He possessed a keen ability to discern wisdom from the written word, often jotting down thoughts and insights that resonated with him. This practice, inherited from his elder brother and father, became a cornerstone of his intellectual and spiritual growth. He, along with his elder brother, curated their father's writings into a published work, preserving his legacy and sharing his wisdom with others.

Their efforts did not stop there. In honor of their father's memory, Dr. Rajinder Singh established a trust at Akal University, dedicated to promoting Sikh heritage and values. Through annual recitations of their father's poems, students are reminded of the rich cultural heritage of sacrifice and martyrdom ingrained in Sikh tradition. These events serve as a light of inspiration, fostering spiritual growth and instilling values that transcend generations.

Dr. Singh takes pride in the legacy he has inherited and seeks to pass it on to future generations. With an innate capacity to recognize and emulate goodness, he has dedicated his life to humanitarian causes, embodying the spirit of selfless service instilled in him by his forebears.

In this continuum of heritage and values, Dr. Rajinder Singh finds fulfillment and purpose. His voyage is a manifestation of the enduring power of family, faith, and tradition, shaping not only his own life but also those of future generations. Through his example, he ensures that the flame of his family's legacy continues to burn brightly, illuminating the path for others to follow. Despite providing his children with the same upbringing, opportunities, and love, he acknowledges that each individual is unique, influenced not only by their environment and genetics but also by intangible factors that defy explanation. Despite the equal distribution of resources and affection within the family, Dr. Singh observes differences between his children that cannot be solely attributed to their upbringing or genetic makeup.

This realization reflects and recognizes the complexity of human nature and the multitude of factors that shape individual identity and character. While environment and genetics play significant roles in shaping a person, there remains an element of mystery in the development of personality, values, and traits.

Dr. Rajinder Singh's experience highlights the limitations of our understanding and the importance of recognizing as well as embracing the inherent diversity among individuals. It serves as a reminder that despite our best efforts to provide equal opportunities and support, each person's journey is uniquely their own, shaped by a combination of known and unknown influences.

In acknowledging the incomprehensible aspects of human nature, Dr. Rajinder Singh reaffirms the importance of acceptance, understanding, and unconditional love within the family. Regardless of differences, fostering an environment of respect, empathy, and support ensures that each individual can flourish and thrive in their own way. He delves into the complexities of human existence, drawing upon Hindu philosophy's concept of *sanskar* to ponder the mysteries of life. *Sanskar* suggests that past experiences and actions carry forward into the present life, influencing individual destinies in ways that are not always readily apparent or understandable.

In his reflections, he observes stark contrasts within families, where despite adverse environments and parental behaviors, some children emerge with values and virtues diametrically opposed to those of their parents. This phenomenon defies easy explanation and challenges conventional understanding.

While environment and upbringing undoubtedly shape individuals to a significant extent, their experiences illustrate that they do not wholly determine one's character or trajectory in life. Despite adverse circumstances, some individuals display resilience, integrity, and moral fortitude that seem to transcend their surroundings.

Dr. Rajinder Singh's musings echo a broader truth: that human existence is multifaceted and mysterious, influenced by a number of factors, some of which may remain beyond our comprehension. While we strive to understand and explain the world around us, there are elements of the human experience that elude rational explanation.

In contemplating the complexities of human nature, Dr. Rajinder Singh emphasizes the importance of humility and openness to the unknown. He acknowledges that while we may not be able to explain everything, we can still strive to live with compassion, empathy, and understanding toward others, recognizing the inherent dignity and worth of every individual, regardless of their circumstances or background.

Dr. Rajinder Singh reflects on the timeless wisdom of Socrates, a towering figure in the history of Greek philosophy. Despite his vast knowledge and intellectual prowess, Socrates humbly asserted that true wisdom lay in acknowledging the limits of one's understanding. This insight, spanning over two millennia, continues to resonate as a reminder of the humility necessary for genuine intellectual inquiry.

Socrates' influence extended far beyond his own time, shaping the teachings of his student Plato and leaving an indelible mark on Western philosophy. His emphasis on the importance of self-awareness and intellectual humility serves as a timeless reminder of the complexities of knowledge and the perpetual quest for truth. Socrates aka Sukraat said, "The only true wisdom is in knowing you know nothing."

In juxtaposition to Socrates' ancient wisdom, Dr. Singh invokes the words of Malala Yousafzai, the youngest Nobel Prize laureate and a symbol of courage and resilience. Malala's poignant observation highlights the transformative power of education in combating ignorance and extremism. Her words, spoken from the perspective of youth and firsthand experience, underline the great impact that education can have in shaping individuals and societies for the better. He recalls her words, "With a gun, you can kill terrorists, with education you can kill terrorism."

For Dr. Rajinder Singh, these words are not mere aphorisms but guiding principles that inspire and uplift. He recognizes the transformative potential of words to change lives and effect positive change in the world. Whether through the teachings of ancient philosophers or the impassioned pleas of modern activists, words possess a unique power to challenge, enlighten, and elevate humanity.

His reverence for the potency of words extends even further, acknowledging the transcendent power of divine praise. In his view, the words sung in reverence to God hold a special significance, transcending human understanding and imbuing life with a deeper spiritual meaning.

As Dr. Rajinder Singh prepares for his workshop or release function, he carries with him the keen insights gleaned from Socrates, Malala, and countless others whose words have left an indelible mark on his own natural life. In celebrating the transformative power of words, he seeks to inspire others to embrace the pursuit of knowledge, wisdom, and spiritual enlightenment.

In the annals of Sikh history, the narrative of Shri Guru Nanak Dev Ji's encounter with the Sidh reverberates with the resonance of spiritual wisdom. When confronted with questions about his guru and his path, Guru Nanak responded with a declaration that transcends time and space:

ਪਵਨ ਆਰੰਭ ਸਤਿਗੁਰ ਮਤ ਵੇਲਾ

ਸਬਦ ਗੁਰੂ ਸੁਰਤਿ ਧੁਨਿ ਚੇਲਾ ॥

"Pawan arambh satguru mat vela, shabad guru surat dhun chala."

From the air came the beginning. This is the age of the True Guru's Teachings.

The Shabad is the Guru, upon whom I lovingly focus my consciousness; I am the Chela, the disciple.

(Shabad is my Guru, and I am the *chela*.)

In this pivotal moment, Guru Nanak encapsulated the essence of Sikh spirituality, emphasizing the primacy of divine revelation over earthly authority. For him, the true guru was not a person or institution but the divine word, the *shabad*, sung in praise of God. This insight laid the foundation for the Sikh tradition, affirming the transformative power of spiritual wisdom and devotion.

The significance of Guru Nanak's words extends beyond mere theological discourse; it carries implications for individual and collective consciousness. By proclaiming the *shabad* as his Guru, Guru Nanak challenged conventional notions of religious hierarchy and sectarianism, inviting seekers of truth to embrace a path guided by inner illumination and divine inspiration.

Guru Nanak's spiritual journey took him far and wide, including a momentous visit to the Kaaba, the holiest site in Islam. Despite the cultural and religious differences, Guru Nanak approached the Kaaba with reverence and humility, positioning his feet toward the revered structure as he rested for the night.

The Qazi, Rukn Ud-Din, alarmed by what he perceived as disrespect toward the sacred site, confronted Guru Nanak with indignation. Yet, Guru Nanak's response was marked by grace and wisdom, surpassing the boundaries of religious dogma and sectarianism. He simply said, "Turn my legs to where God is not present," prompting a miraculous revelation that left the Qazi awestruck.

In that transformative moment, the Qazi's heart was touched, and his soul was stirred by the power of Guru Nanak's presence and the divine message he embodied. Through dialog and exchange, Guru Nanak and the Qazi engaged in a heartfelt spiritual discourse, transcending linguistic and cultural barriers to explore the deeper mysteries of existence.

Moved by Guru Nanak's teachings and the spiritual resonance of the *shabad*, the Qazi underwent a deep change, embracing Sikhism and becoming a devoted disciple of Guru Nanak. His journey from skepticism to faith, from hostility to reverence, exemplifies the transformative power of spiritual wisdom and the universal appeal of divine truth.

However, the Qazi's conversion did not go unnoticed by the authorities, who viewed it as a threat to their religious orthodoxy. In a tragic turn of events, the Qazi faced persecution and ultimately martyrdom for his newfound faith. Yet, even in the face of persecution and death, his firm devotion to Guru Nanak and the *shabad* remained steadfast, affirming the enduring power of faith and the triumph of the human spirit over adversity. Rukn Ud-Din is recorded in history as the first Sikh martyr.

The story of Rukn Ud-Din Qazi serves as a poignant reminder of the power of words and the transformative potential of spiritual wisdom. In a world often divided by religious and ideological differences, Guru Nanak's teachings offer a timeless message of unity, compassion, and spiritual liberation. As we navigate the complexities of life, may we heed the wisdom of Guru Nanak and embrace the transformative power of the divine word, the *shabad*, as our eternal Guru.

Dr. Rajinder Singh says they are so powerful that they can change your life totally. "Whatever we say, it becomes our habit, one can say. Then, the habit becomes the character; the character becomes destiny; and destiny is your life, ultimately!"

ਸਚਹੁ ਓਰੈ ਸਭੁ ਕੋ ਉਪਰਿ ਸਚੁ ਆਚਾਰੁ ॥5॥

Sri Guru Granth Sahib Page: 62

Sacho Urey Sab Ko Upper Sach Achar.

Dr. Rajinder says he is thoroughly impressed by the thinkers and philosophers of the world who have made very far-sighted statements, which are centuries old but still immensely relevant today.

The truth is at the top and everything is below it. Above the truth is *Achar*. Above the truth, there is a virtuous life. Your character. *Achar* means conduct, behavior, and character. Truth is the highest thing. Truth is God. Your life is higher than this. This is the exact word. So, it is most important to have a virtuous life and then probably you will be blessed by everyone. Our aim in life is to accumulate blessings and good wishes from all and do *Simran* and *Seva* (meditation on God's name and selfless service to humanity) so that we attain the purpose for which we were born. Dr. Singh has been practicing this philosophy and has gotten the desired results too.

He eloquently expresses his deep-seated belief in the transformative power of words and values, reflecting on the impact they have on shaping individual lives and destinies. He emphasizes that words are not merely uttered but become ingrained in our habits, ultimately shaping our character and determining our destiny.

Drawing inspiration from the timeless wisdom of philosophers and thinkers across the ages, he emphasizes the enduring relevance of their insights in the present day. He finds solace and guidance in their statements, which continue to resonate with truth and insight, despite the passage of centuries.

Central to Dr. Rajinder Singh's philosophy is the earnest teaching of Guru Nanak Sahib, who declared that truth reigns supreme above all else. He emphasized the importance of leading a virtuous life, guided by principles of honesty, integrity, and compassion. For him, this is not just a philosophical concept but a guiding principle that is central to every aspect of his life.

In his pursuit of a virtuous life, Dr. Rajinder Singh seeks to accumulate the blessings and good wishes of others, recognizing the importance of humility, service, and devotion in achieving spiritual fulfillment. He places great value on the practice of *Simran* (remembrance of the divine) and *Seva* (selfless service), seeing them as essential pathways to realizing one's true purpose in life.

Through his adherence to these timeless values and principles, he has found fulfillment and success in both his personal and professional endeavors. His firm vow to truth, virtue, and spiritual growth serves as a light of inspiration for others seeking to lead meaningful and purposeful lives.

In essence, Dr. Rajinder Singh's philosophy is one of acute simplicity and timeless wisdom. It is rooted in the belief that by aligning oneself with the highest principles of truth and virtue, one can transcend the limitations of worldly existence and attain a state of spiritual fulfillment and inner peace.

He reflects on his life with gratitude, recognizing the blessings that have shaped his life. He attributes his success and fulfillment not to his own efforts alone but to the abundant blessings he has received. For him, the accumulation of values and virtues is the ultimate aim of life, guiding his daily practice and shaping his worldview.

Dr. Rajinder Singh observes the uniqueness of each individual, acknowledging the diversity of human nature and behavior. He reflects on the harmonious relationship between his parents, noting his father's support and his mother's resilience in the face of challenges. Despite differences among his siblings, he appreciates the rare phenomenon of his father's gentle and nurturing approach, which fostered a sense of contentment and gratitude within the family.

His father's perspective on life, characterized by contentment and gratitude, left a lasting impression on him. He learned that true happiness stems not from external circumstances but from an attitude of gratitude and appreciation for life's blessings. Dr. Rajinder internalized his father's belief that gratitude precedes happiness, shaping his own outlook on life and influencing his interactions with others.

Dr. Singh emphasizes the transformative power of attitude and perspective, noting that one's thoughts can shape their reality. He believes that by cultivating a positive mindset and embracing gratitude, individuals can unlock their full potential and lead fulfilling lives. For him, the fundamental principle is that thoughts are paramount, and by changing one's thoughts, one can change one's life.

In essence, his philosophy revolves around the connection between gratitude, attitude, and happiness. By embracing a mindset of gratitude and cultivating positive thoughts, individuals can navigate life's challenges with resilience and find true fulfillment in the richness of the human experience. He says he thinks he is the most fortunate person to be where he is today. This is all due to the blessings of his elders and people around him, and not his doing. The accumulation of values and virtues should be the aim of life.

Dr. Singh says he has been trying to practice this every day. Each individual is unique. Everyone is different. His brothers are different from him. His father used to say he had five Shravan Kumars in the form of five sons.

He believes it's not happiness that brings gratitude. It is the gratitude that brings happiness, and he was always blessed with more than what he deserved.

He reflects on the lessons learned from the enduring bond between his parents, particularly the support his father provided to his mother during times of adversity. Witnessing his father's steadfast loyalty left a lasting impression on him, shaping his own values and approach to relationships.

In his own marriage, he consciously practiced the same principles of loyalty and support that he witnessed in his parents' relationship. He understood the importance of standing by his partner through life's challenges, just as his father had stood by his mother. His vow to his wife mirrored the deep-seated values instilled in him by his upbringing, fostering a strong and enduring bond built on mutual respect and firm support.

By emulating the example set by his parents, Dr. Rajinder Singh cultivated a relationship characterized by love, understanding, and resilience. His marriage became a testament to the enduring power of loyalty and promise, affirming the impact that parental role models can have on shaping one's own approach to relationships and life.

Dr. Singh shares a deeply troubling account of a colleague facing a serious illness and abandonment by her husband. Despite their shared medical expertise, the husband chose to neglect his wife during her time of need, even going so far as to seek a divorce to pursue a relationship with another woman.

This heartbreaking situation exemplifies a stark departure from the values of compassion, loyalty, and support that Dr. Rajinder Singh holds dear. He laments the erosion of moral integrity and selflessness in today's society, where individuals prioritize their own interests above the well-being of others, even those closest to them.

His narrative emphasizes the harsh reality of a world increasingly driven by materialism and self-interest, where relationships are discarded, and values are disregarded in pursuit of personal gain. He expresses deep sorrow at witnessing such callousness and selfishness, particularly in individuals who hold positions of authority.

Despite the despair evoked by this tale, Dr. Rajinder remains resolute in his conviction to uphold the values of compassion, empathy, and integrity in his own life. He recognizes the importance of individual contributions in fostering a more compassionate and empathetic society, even in the face of overwhelming indifference and apathy.

Ultimately, his narrative serves as a poignant reminder of the enduring importance of kindness, empathy, and moral integrity in navigating the complexities of human relationships and societal dynamics. In a world fraught with challenges and moral ambiguities, it is incumbent upon individuals to strive for compassion and decency in their interactions with others, lest we lose sight of our shared humanity.

He reflects on the diminishing presence of values in contemporary society, attributing this trend to the lack of emphasis on value-based education during childhood. He observes that parents and teachers play a pivotal role in instilling values in children, but the pervasive influence of materialism often overshadows these efforts. He acknowledges the challenges faced in rural areas, where access to quality education and resources may be limited, yet he finds hope in organizations like The Kalgidhar Trust, which are dedicated to imparting value-based education in rural communities.

Despite the prevailing materialistic mindset, Dr. Singh remains steadfast in his belief that the higher purpose of life is to serve others. He emphasizes the importance of altruism and selflessness in leading a meaningful existence, rejecting the notion that life is solely about self-interest or the welfare of one's loved ones. For him, true fulfillment lies in dedicating oneself to the welfare of others, transcending personal ambitions and pursuits.

Dr. Rajinder traces his own life toward altruism, noting the various stages of his career and personal development that ultimately led him to prioritize service to others. While he pursued education and career advancement, he gradually realized the significance of selfless service and found the courage to redirect his life's path toward this noble endeavor. For him, this shift represented a transformative moment of enlightenment, a conscious decision to prioritize the welfare of others above personal gain.

In sharing his story, Dr. Rajinder Singh offers insight into the transformative power of altruism and the capacity for individuals to find meaning and purpose through service to others. He encourages others to reflect on their own values and aspirations, recognizing the inherent fulfillment that comes from acts of kindness and compassion. Despite the challenges and obstacles that may arise, his time serves as proof of the enduring importance of altruism in navigating life's complexities and finding true fulfillment in the service of others.

Reflecting on his own life, Dr. Rajinder Singh recalls his years of service in the army and civil life, during which he felt limited in his ability to contribute to society. However, upon retiring in 1991, along with his wife, Dr. Savitri R. Singh, he took proactive steps to address societal needs by establishing a polyclinic named Bhai Kahnhaiya dispensary at their local gurdwara. This initiative, which has been running for over three decades, provides free healthcare services and consultations to the public, thanks to the staunch support of numerous specialists and super-specialists who volunteer their services.

Dr. Savitri R. Singh played a pivotal role in initiating this noble endeavor, demonstrating her loyalty to serving the community and addressing healthcare disparities. Her proactive approach exemplifies the values of compassion, generosity, and altruism that Dr. Singh advocates for in society. Through their collective efforts, they have made a tangible impact on the lives of those in need, embodying the principles of selflessness and service that they hold dear.

In sharing this story, he highlights the importance of taking proactive steps to uphold values and address societal needs, even in the face of prevailing materialism and indifference. He encourages others to follow their example by finding ways to contribute positively to their communities, thereby fostering a culture of compassion, generosity, and mutual support. His narrative serves as a reminder of the transformative power of altruism and the enduring impact of selfless acts of kindness on individuals and society as a whole.

Dr. Rajinder Singh acknowledges the pivotal role his wife played in setting the course of his life. He attests that it was indeed she who initiated their drive by establishing the polyclinic at the gurdwara. Initially, Dr. Savitri R. Singh, a versatile physician trained in general medicine and gynecology, began providing medical care to the local community. Over time, as patient demand grew, he also became involved in the endeavor.

Driven by the needs of their patients and the desire to provide comprehensive healthcare services, the clinic expanded to include specialists in various medical fields, such as ophthalmology, otolaryngology, dermatology, psychiatry, and more. Today, their clinic stands as one of the premier healthcare facilities in North India, offering a wide range of medical services, including laboratory testing, dental care, and free medicines.

Dr. Singh's initiative into community service was catalyzed by his wife's compassionate and proactive approach to healthcare. Her support in addressing the healthcare needs of the community inspired him to join her in this noble endeavor. Together, they have created a legacy of service that continues to positively impact the lives of countless individuals in their community. Through their collaborative efforts, they have built a flare of hope and healing, embodying the values of selflessness and compassion for the well-being of others.

Dr. Rajinder Singh also proudly highlights the invaluable contributions of philanthropist Dr. S.P.S. Oberoi to their healthcare initiatives. His generosity significantly enhanced the services offered at their clinic, particularly in the fields of radiology, laboratory diagnostics, dental care, and physiotherapy. Dr. Oberoi's substantial financial support has enabled the establishment and operation of these essential departments, ensuring that patients receive comprehensive and high-quality care. He also shared that S. Tejwant Singh Gill, the president of the Gurdwara Shri Teg Bahadur Sahib Ji, has put in steadfast and highly appreciable efforts for constructing an advanced new building of Bhai Kanhaiya Dispensary.

Despite being a successful businessman based in Dubai, Dr. Oberoi exemplifies the Sikh tradition of philanthropy by generously allocating a significant portion of his income to humanitarian causes. His pledge to give back extends beyond the customary 10 percent, with Dr. Oberoi contributing an astounding 98 percent of his earnings to charitable causes. This extraordinary level of generosity reflects his deep-seated compassion for making a positive impact on the lives of others.

Dr. Oberoi's philanthropic efforts have garnered international recognition, with numerous prestigious awards and accolades honoring his selfless contributions to society. His dedication to humanitarian causes extends beyond healthcare, as evidenced by his pivotal role in securing clemency for 17 individuals facing capital punishment in Dubai. Dr. Oberoi's intervention saved the lives of these individuals, transcending religious and cultural divides to uphold the sanctity of human life.

Dr. Oberoi's philanthropic endeavors have elevated the status of both the Sikh community and the nation as a whole. His dedication to serving others has not only enhanced the well-being of individuals in need but has also highlighted the importance of altruism and compassion in society. He highlights the teachings of their guru, which emphasize serving others, a principle that Dr. Oberoi has wholeheartedly embraced in his actions.

Dr. Rajinder Singh emphasizes the significance of daily prayer in Sikh tradition, particularly the invocation for blessings of service and remembrance. He explains that this prayer seeks the wealth of service to others and the remembrance of the divine, aiming for spiritual liberation. Through the practice of singing praises and serving others, individuals aspire to attain spiritual fulfillment and liberation from worldly attachments.

In the Sikh tradition, the *Ardas*, or supplication, is a crucial aspect of daily prayer. Dr. Singh highlights the importance of the *Ardas*, reciting the last words:

Soi piyade mel

Jin Milya, Tera Naam chit aave

Nanak Naam Chardi Kala

Tere Bhaane Sarta da Bhlaa

Bless me, O Lord, so that I am able to render selfless service and meditate on Your Name and grace me with the accomplishment of human life. Also, bestow upon me the association of those meeting whom I remember Your Name.

Nanak Nam Chardi Kala

Tere Bhaane Sarbat Da Bhala

Reciting Your Name Nanak remains cheerful and buoyant and seeks your blessing of well-being to descend on everyone.

Dr. Singh emphasizes the impact of words and environment on individuals, noting that what one hears and surrounds oneself with can significantly influence one's thoughts and actions. He stresses the importance of cultivating a value-based and positive environment to nurture spiritual growth and well-being.

Dr. Rajinder Singh, with his wisdom and hope for the youth of Punjab, envisioned a future where the scourge of addiction would be replaced by a culture of empowerment and enlightenment. His vision is rooted in the rich heritage of Punjab's ethos and the teachings of the revered Sri Guru Granth Sahib Ji.

Understanding that true education transcends mere literacy, he emphasized the importance of instilling moral and spiritual values in the youth. He believes that education devoid of values could only lead to egoism and self-centeredness, perpetuating the cycle of societal decay.

Drawing from the wisdom of the founding saints, he outlined the three pillars of education: literacy, values, and selfless service. He believed that literacy, when combined with moral and spiritual values, transformed individuals into compassionate and responsible members of society.

For Dr. Singh, spiritual enlightenment was not confined to the walls of institutions but was a crusade of self-reflection and connection with one's spiritual heritage. He advocated for the establishment of Gurukuls, where the youth could cultivate a deep reverence for their values and traditions.

At Akal Academy, Baru Sahib, Dr. Neelam Kaur (his daughter) and her team are dedicated to nurturing the holistic development of the youth. They believe that by equipping the youth with tools of knowledge, morality, and spirituality, they could overcome the grip of addiction and pave the way for a brighter future for Punjab.

In his vision, the youth of Punjab were not just passive recipients of education but active agents of change, empowered to create a society based on compassion, empathy, and harmony. It is a vision that inspired hope and ignited a sense of purpose among the youth as they embarked on an effort of introspection and service to their communities.

Sikh Gurus' spiritual wisdom is universal. It applies to all, regardless of caste, creed, color, gender, age, and religion. But it is sad to note that a large number of Sikh children are not motivated enough to follow Sikh values. Many young people are addicted to alcohol, drugs, substance abuse, and social media due to prevalent societal fashion or peer pressure. Unfortunately, Sikhs are ignoring this facet of their community life. However, there is no shortage of available opportunities that can help Sikh youth avoid this awful situation. The only condition is that we must reorient our outlook and actions.

Chapter 8

Abiding Legacy

Dr. Rajinder Singh carries a deep understanding of the struggles and sacrifices made by his mother throughout her life. Despite facing significant challenges, including physical and mental health issues, she persevered for the sake of her family. Her experiences, particularly the difficulties she endured due to strained relationships within the family, left a lasting impact on him.

From his mother, he inherited resilience and desirelessness. He learned firsthand the importance of compassion and support, especially during times of adversity. Her desire for her children to be born during winter, as they didn't have the means to tackle the summer, a time when she felt most isolated and neglected, highlights her longing for warmth and connection amidst hardship.

His mother's life serves as a poignant reminder of the complexities of family dynamics and the enduring strength found in the face of adversity. Her legacy lives on through her son's compassion, understanding, and healing. He reflects on her simplicity in his life.

The story of Shri Guru Tegh Bahadur Ji's sacrifice for the Kashmiri Pandits is a fine example of selflessness and courage, which impacted Dr. Singh. When the Kashmiri Pandits sought refuge and protection from religious persecution, Guru Tegh Bahadur fearlessly stood against oppression, even at the cost of his own life.

Despite being approached by Mughal Emperor Aurangzeb with the offer of conversion to Islam to spare his life, Guru Tegh Bahadur remained steadfast in his principles and refused to compromise his faith. He understood the gravity of the situation and willingly embraced martyrdom to uphold the freedom of religion and protect the rights of the oppressed.

Guru Tegh Bahadur's sacrifice resonates as a symbol of resistance against tyranny and an illustration of the enduring spirit of humanity. His legacy continues to inspire generations with its message of compassion, courage, and a spirit of justice.

Dr. Singh's father's admiration for the Akali Morcha, the nonviolent movement launched by the Sikhs in the 1920s to liberate their gurdwaras from corrupt *mahants*, speaks volumes about his values and beliefs. Despite his limited formal education, he recognized the significance of the struggle for justice and was deeply inspired by the sacrifices made by the Sikh community during that time.

The Akali Morcha was a pivotal moment in Sikh history, symbolizing the relentless pursuit of righteousness and the defense of religious freedom. The Sikhs' pledge to non-violence and their resolve in the face of adversity resonated with Dr. Singh.

His reverence for the Akali Morcha influenced his own principles and actions, instilling in him a sense of duty toward fighting against injustice and advocating for the rights of the oppressed. His admiration for this historical movement reflects the enduring impact of courageous acts of resistance and the power of collective action in the pursuit of a just society.

Also, Dr. Singh's father's deep admiration for the nonviolent principles and his connection to Sikh history and values shine through his actions and creative endeavors. Despite his limited formal education, his understanding of the importance of nonviolent resistance and his appreciation for the sacrifices made by the Sikh community during the liberation of gurdwaras demonstrate his moral integrity and sense of justice.

The atrocities committed by the oppressors at Nankana Sahib and elsewhere served as powerful catalysts for his father's creative expression. His decision to write poems about these events reflects his desire to preserve and honor the memory of those who suffered and died for their faith. By translating his writings into Punjabi and publishing them, Dr. Rajinder Singh ensured that the stories of resilience and courage would be passed down through generations, inspiring others to uphold noble values and resist oppression.

Dr. Singh's father's firm loyalty to 'Gurmat' and his embodiment of noble values in his own life speaks volumes about his character and legacy. His dedication to preserving Sikh history and promoting non-violence serves as an example of his enduring impact on those around him as well as the broader community.

The legacy left by Dr. Singh's parents and elder brother is one of major inspiration, guidance, and integrity. Their values, principles, and the examples they set have undoubtedly shaped who Dr. Rajinder Singh is today. Despite the pressures and challenges faced, he remained resolute in his beliefs and stood firm in his convictions, reflecting the strength of character instilled by his mentors.

Their legacy goes beyond material possessions. As he rightly points out, "While some may focus on tangible wealth or assets, the true legacy lies in the intangible qualities, i.e., values and principles passed down through generations. The courage to uphold truth and integrity in the face of adversity, the strong desire for noble values, and the undying support and guidance are my family's legacy."

In essence, the legacy left by his parents and brother is proof of the power of values and moral courage. It serves as a guiding light for future generations, reminding us all of the importance of staying true to our values and principles, even in the face of adversity.

Dr. Rajinder Singh's daughter, Dr. Neelam Kaur's pure intent for social service and her dedication to following in the footsteps of her family's legacy are commendable. Despite the challenges and obligations, such as her mother's work and other factors that may have hindered consistency, she remained inspired by the values instilled by her father and mother.

Her investment in social service, particularly soon after marriage, reflects her deep-rooted sense of duty and compassion. Through her actions, she is carrying forward the legacy of service and altruism established by her family, leaving a positive impact on her community and setting a powerful example for her own children.

The success and achievements of Dr. Rajinder Singh's accomplished grand-daughters, both highly qualified and well-placed, are an illustration of the values and education imparted by the parents and their family legacy. Their education at Akal Academy, Baru Sahib, shows the importance of quality education in shaping individuals who contribute meaningfully to society. His eldest granddaughter's achievements in the medical field, coupled with her selflessness and dedication to her profession, are truly inspiring. Her willingness to travel long distances daily for her work, despite the considerable expenses involved, demonstrates her commitment to making a difference in the lives of others, regardless of personal inconvenience or financial considerations.

Similarly, Dr. Singh's younger granddaughter's pursuit of a PhD in economics and her thoughtful approach to financial matters reflect a strong sense of responsibility and prudence. Both granddaughters embody the values of diligence, dedication, and compassion instilled by their family.

While their approaches to their careers may differ, their shared duty to their studies, their professions, their faith, and their service to society highlights the enduring legacy of integrity, values, and academic pursuit passed down through the generations.

Dr. Singh's gratitude for his grandchildren's achievements and character indicates the impact of familial influence and the blessings bestowed upon him by a loving and supportive family. Indeed, the wonders of God's grace and the intricate complexities of human nature defy simple explanations, reminding us of the depth and richness of life's mysteries.

His post-retirement endeavors are evidence of his ongoing resolve to serve his community and make a positive impact in the field of healthcare and mental well-being. His dedication to sharing his insights and wisdom through writing, culminating in the publication of 'Gems of Wisdom' showcases his desire to inspire and uplift others.

Additionally, his involvement in running the Bhai Kanhaiya Dispensary, started by his late wife over three decades ago, reflects his deep-rooted compassion and dedication to providing free medical services to those in need. The dispensary's comprehensive range of services, including consultations with specialists and the provision of free medications, highlights his assurance to address various healthcare needs within the community.

Furthermore, his involvement in managing de-addiction centers in Punjab and Himachal Pradesh marks his dedication to combating substance abuse and promoting mental health and well-being. The establishment of these centers, providing essential services in rural areas, demonstrates Dr. Singh's vision for creating accessible and effective solutions to address societal challenges.

His post-retirement achievements represent a continuation of his lifelong dedication to serving others and making a difference in the lives of those around him. His efforts in healthcare and community service serve as an inspiration to others and leave a lasting legacy of compassion and generosity to social welfare.

Dr. Rajinder Singh's reflection on his life's work highlights a deep sense of gratitude and fulfillment. He attributes his achievements not solely to his own efforts but to the blessings and guidance he received from spiritual figures like Sant Baba Iqbal Singh Ji. Inspired by his call to address the issue of drug addiction and provide value-based education, he embarked on a mission to make a difference in his community.

Through his tireless efforts and dedication, he has established significant healthcare initiatives, including de-addiction centers and dispensaries, to address the pressing needs of those affected by substance abuse and other health issues. His dedication to serving others and his belief in the power of compassion and service reflect the legacy of Sant Baba Iqbal Singh Ji and the teachings of Sikhism.

The legacy of Sant Atar Singh Ji and his successors, including Sant Teja Singh Ji, Dr. Khem Singh, and Sant Baba Iqbal Singh, is indeed wonderful. Their collective efforts have led to the establishment of 129 Akal Academies and two universities, which have brought about a revolution in education in rural areas across North India.

These academies represent more than just educational institutions; they embody a holistic approach to education that integrates modern learning with timeless spiritual values. By instilling moral and ethical principles alongside academic knowledge, these academies have been guiding students toward a path of personal growth, social responsibility, and spiritual enlightenment.

The emphasis on value-based education reflects a deep understanding of the importance of nurturing not only the intellect but also the heart and soul. By imparting spiritual wisdom and moral teachings, these academies are not only shaping the minds of future generations but also fostering a sense of purpose, compassion, and integrity in students.

The legacy of Sant Atar Singh Ji Mustuana and his successors is a testament to the power of education to uplift communities and inspire positive change. Through their visionary leadership and intent on serving humanity, they have left an indelible mark on the landscape of education in India, paving the way for a brighter and more enlightened future.

Dr. Rajinder Singh's perspective on his legacy reflects a deep sense of humility and contentment. He does not concern himself with whether future generations will remember his contributions or not. Instead, he emphasizes the importance of fulfilling one's duty and leaving a positive impact to the best of one's abilities.

He believes that striving for recognition or remembrance is not essential. He sees his efforts as a humble attempt to make a difference, regardless of whether they are remembered or not. He encourages a mindset of gratitude and contentment, focusing on the present moment rather than expectations for the future.

Furthermore, he highlights the importance of managing expectations to avoid stress and discontent. He shares the wisdom passed down by his father, advocating for setting ambitious goals but finding contentment in whatever one achieves.

Ultimately, his legacy is not defined by external recognition or remembrance but by the values he embodies and the impact he has had on those around him. His emphasis on humility, gratitude, and contentment serves as a guiding principle for living a fulfilling and meaningful life, regardless of its remembrance by future generations.

Dr. Singh believes that true happiness comes from within and is not contingent upon recognition or remembrance. His emphasis on gratitude and contentment reflects a deep understanding of the human experience. His humility and wisdom shine through his words, inspiring others to find peace in the present moment. His legacy is a witness to the power of living with purpose and integrity, leaving a lasting imprint on those fortunate enough to encounter his wisdom.

"I believe that true fulfillment comes from within, not from external recognition or remembrance. Happiness is found in gratitude and contentment for life's blessings. My legacy, if any, lies in the sincerity of my actions and the depth of my character. I strive to live authentically, guided by love, kindness, and self-reflection. Through humility and wisdom, I hope to inspire others to find joy in the present moment and live with purpose and integrity," he shares.

Now, as he nears a deeper understanding of spirituality, Dr. Rajinder Singh emphasizes the importance of managing expectations and finding contentment in life's blessings. He believes that happiness stems from gratefulness, and one cannot be truly happy without first being grateful. This perspective shapes his outlook on life and influences his approach to challenges and adversity. He believes, "I cannot count the blessings of Waheguru, the more I count, **the more they multiply, reminding me of His infinite grace and mercy.**"

Ultimately, his legacy is one of humility, gratitude, and a deep appreciation for life's complete cycle. His insights and wisdom serve as guiding principles for living a meaningful and fulfilling life, leaving a lasting impression on those who have the privilege of hearing his words.

Nowadays, Dr. Rajinder Singh finds solace and fulfillment in his seemingly non-existent free time. Engaging in activities such as reading newspapers, delving into books that pique his interest, and jotting down notes of noteworthy content. His quirky habit of transcribing articles even after they have been published showcases his deep-rooted dedication to learning and documentation. He fondly shares that he has filled almost one more book with his notes and readings.

Patient consultations have continued up to the age of 91 years in his current routine. He frequently receives calls from drug de-addiction centers, either from Sangrur or Baru Sahib, mainly from patients who insist on seeing him specifically. Despite his age, with continued efforts to address the issues of patients, his dedication to his profession remains undisturbed.

He often quotes the following lines enshrined in Sri Guru Granth Sahib Ji about *seva* or volunteering:

One who performs selfless service, without thought of reward,

shall attain his Lord and Master.

In the narrative of Dr. Rajinder Singh's life, the overarching theme is one of service and sacrifice to make a positive impact on society. His life, spanning decades of dedication to his profession and community, is the finest example of the enduring values of compassion, humility, and the relentless pursuit of knowledge.

At the heart of his legacy lies a deep-seated desire to alleviate suffering and promote well-being.

Throughout his career, Dr. Rajinder Singh has remained true to his principles, never wavering in the face of challenges or setbacks. His will to provide quality healthcare, regardless of one's ability to pay, accentuates his belief in the fundamental right to health and dignity. By establishing polyclinics and de-addiction centers, he has ensured that marginalized communities have access to essential medical services, thereby empowering them to lead healthier, more fulfilling lives.

Despite facing adversity and personal challenges, he has remained steadfast in his duty to serve others, drawing strength from his faith and the support of his family. His optimism and belief in the inherent goodness of humanity serve as a lighthouse of hope in an often tumultuous world.

Chapter 9

A Life Well Lived

Dr. Rajinder Singh's influence extends even to higher education institutions, where he has played a crucial role in assisting 16 vice-chancellors of Himachal Pradesh universities in establishing mental health cells. These cells serve as essential resources for promoting mental health awareness and support within academic communities.

Through his guidance and expertise, he has helped create environments where mental health is prioritized, providing students and faculty members with the resources and support they need to address mental health concerns effectively. By nurturing these mental health cells, he has demonstrated his undying will to shape future generations of healthcare professionals who are equipped to address the complex challenges of mental health in their respective fields.

Despite retiring from the armed forces, Dr. Rajinder Singh's dedication to humanitarian causes remained steadfast. He continued his service to humanity through voluntary work, particularly at the Guru Tegh Bahadur Gurdwara in Sector 34, Chandigarh. He is recognized as the oldest and most senior doctor providing voluntary service at the gurdwara's dispensary, established by his late wife, Dr. Savitri R. Singh, in 1991.

As the number of patients seeking medical assistance grew, additional rooms were constructed to accommodate the expanding services. Separate rooms were designated for allopathic, ayurvedic, and homeopathic doctors, along with facilities for injection and dressing work. In January 2009, the Gujral family of Sector 33 Chandigarh, donated funds for a laboratory equipped with automatic testing machines, enhancing the diagnostic capabilities of the dispensary.

Over time, the dispensary expanded its services further, incorporating a dental department in mid-1996, followed by ayurvedic treatment in mid-1997, and the introduction of X-ray and laboratory facilities in early 1998. Additionally, a physiotherapy department was established in 1998.

Dr. Savitri R. Singh dedicated her evenings from 6 to 8 pm to ensure uninterrupted medical services at the dispensary. Regardless of festivals or holidays, including Diwali, Dussehra, and Gurpurabs, the dispensary remained open, and no registration fee was charged from patients, many of whom belonged to low-economic backgrounds, such as laborers and domestic helpers and their families.

Following Dr. Savitri R. Singh's sudden demise in September 2000, a medical officer was employed to attend to patients regularly. However, Dr. Rajinder Singh and other doctors continue to provide voluntary services at the dispensary, carrying forward Dr. Savitri R. Singh's legacy of compassionate care for the underprivileged.

From its humble beginnings with just one room and a single doctor, the dispensary at one time expanded to include 13 rooms and a team of 36 specialized doctors offering a wide range of medical services. These doctors, with qualifications such as MD,

MS, FRCS, FRCP, MDS, and DM, cover various specialties, including internal medicine, psychiatry, geriatrics, ophthalmology, otorhinolaryngology (ENT), gynecology, and dermatology. In addition to the medical staff, there are pharmacy managers, laboratory technicians, radiography technicians, EEG technicians, PAP smear technicians, dental department staff, and others.

Starting in the 1990s, free medical camps have been organized at the Akal Charitable Hospital in Baru Sahib by The Kalgidhar Trust, attracting patients from local areas as well as neighboring states like Punjab, Haryana, and Uttar Pradesh. These camps provided not only medical treatment but also free food, boarding, and lodging for the patients and their families. Volunteer doctors from Punjab and abroad offered their services, covering various specialties, including general medicine, ENT, ophthalmology, psychiatry, cardiology, orthopedics, gynecology, and obstetrics. During these camps, approximately 80 to 90 surgeries were performed, whereas the quality of medical services in the rural areas of Sirmaur District was negligible.

In 2004, Sant Baba Iqbal Singh Ji expressed concern about the growing issue of drug addiction, prompted by appeals from devotees in Punjab. Responding to this call, Baba Ji tasked Dr. Rajinder Singh with establishing a drug de-addiction center in Punjab. The location was chosen in the premises of Gurdwara Janam Asthan Sant Attar Singh at Cheema Sahib, where the first drug de-addiction facility was established by The Kalgidhar Trust, Baru Sahib. Despite the logistical challenges, Dr. Rajinder Singh managed and treated patients single-handedly, commuting from Chandigarh to Cheema and back twice a week.

Dr. Singh's endeavor at the drug de-addiction center in Cheema Sahib saw significant collaborations and expansions. In 2005, he was joined by Mr. Onkar Singh, a psychologist who had previously worked with Dr. Singh at the Red Cross drug de-addiction center in Mohali in the early 1990s. Together, they would visit Cheema Sahib to serve the patients.

During an international psychiatrists' conference in Chandigarh, Dr. Sukhwinder Singh, a psychiatrist residing in the USA, originally from Punjab, learned about Dr. Rajinder Singh's work and the contributions of The Kalgidhar Trust institutions in Baru Sahib. Impressed by their efforts, Dr. Sukhwinder Singh offered his services as a consultant psychiatrist at the Cheema Sahib's de-addiction center.

Another valuable addition to the team was Dr. Sarinda, a doctor from Germany motivated by her personal experience with a family member's struggle with drug addiction. She joined the center with a strong commitment to improving the lives of addiction patients, often emphasizing the importance of understanding their struggles firsthand.

As the center expanded its services, Mr. Onkar Singh increased his responsibility from two days a week to four. In 2006-2007, with divine blessings and Dr. Rajinder Singh's dedicated efforts, a separate building was constructed near Gurdwara Janam Asthan Sant Attar Singh Ji at Cheema Sahib exclusively for the treatment of drug addiction patients. This new facility provided both inpatient and outpatient services. From 2004 until the construction of the center was completed (in 2007), the patients were consulted and treated at the Gurdwara Sahib itself and the community center in Jharon village.

In 2011, when government licensing became necessary for operating drug de-addiction centers, Dr. Rajinder Singh ensured that all required formalities were completed. Under his guidance, the center evolved into a 30-bed facility, further advancing its capacity to serve people in need.

The Akal Drug De-Addiction and Rehabilitation Centres provide comprehensive facilities for all types of drug and alcohol dependence issues at affordable rates. Dr. Rajinder Singh spearheaded the establishment of another center at Baru Sahib in 2016, managed by The Kalgidhar Trust, which also offers specialized treatment for female patients suffering from drug addiction.

A unique aspect of treatment at these centers is the integration of modern medical and psychological approaches with spirituality. Patients are encouraged to embrace spiritual practices, such as morning prayers and meditation, alongside medical treatment. This holistic approach focuses not only on addressing the physical aspects of addiction but also on nurturing the patient's spiritual well-being.

Dr. Singh's visionary leadership in holistic healing has contributed to the success of these centers, with an impressive success rate of around 60%. His efforts have had an impact on individuals and communities affected by addiction, bringing about positive changes and fostering hope for recovery.

Since retiring from the army, Dr. Singh has positively impacted around 10,000 families affected by drug addiction. As the director of both centers, he continues to lead efforts to combat addiction in Punjab and Himachal Pradesh, demonstrating his unswerving duty to improve mental health and addiction recovery. His legacy serves as a reminder of the influence one individual can have on the well-being of others.

Dr. Rajinder Singh humbly praises the Lord for the achievements by citing:

You make the unworthy ones worthy, O my Lord of the Universe;
I am a sacrifice to Your Almighty creative power.

Sri Guru Granth Sahib, Page: 624

Dr. Rajinder Singh's influence extends far beyond addiction recovery, as he now oversees the mental health of 70,000 children enrolled in 129 Akal Academy schools throughout North India. This significant responsibility reflects his dedication to nurturing the well-being of the next generation and his vision for a healthier, happier society. By prioritizing mental health in education, he contributes to building a foundation for the holistic development of young minds, ensuring they have the support and resources needed to thrive academically, emotionally, and socially. His work on the well-being of children underlines his enduring impact on society and exemplifies his staunch dedication to serving others.

Dr. Rajinder Singh, the esteemed founder and director of Akal Drug De-Addiction Centres, displays an unmistakable dedication to the welfare of patients grappling with drug addiction. Despite being 91 years old, he remains deeply committed to ensuring the smooth functioning of the centers, often facing challenges when doctors and staff members take leave or resign. He willingly travels between Baru Sahib in Himachal Pradesh and Cheema Sahib in the Sangrur district of Punjab to provide treatment to patients, even amidst personal health concerns requiring treatment in Chandigarh.

However, bureaucratic obstacles arise, particularly in Sangrur, where local health authorities resist accommodating telepsychiatry sessions for patients in the absence of the appointed psychiatrist. This resistance stems from a dubious alliance and government policies that oppose the ethical delivery of drug de-addiction and mental health services.

Despite the clear benefits of telepsychiatry in ensuring continuity of care, an unjust letter issued by the higher medical authorities on March 9, 2023, restricted the center in Cheema Sahib from admitting patients or prescribing medication without the physical presence of a psychiatrist. This overlooks the rights of patients to receive timely treatment, even when a psychiatrist is available online.

This situation deepens the urgent need for reform within local health authorities to prioritize patient welfare over bureaucratic barriers and dubious alliances. It is imperative that individuals battling addiction receive the care they deserve, irrespective of administrative impediments.

This letter from a higher authority obviously overlooks the right of patients to get treatment even as the psychiatrist is available online via a telepsychiatry facility in the absence of the psychiatrist who has proceeded on a short leave.

Irked by the tone and tenor of the letter, Dr. Rajinder Singh decided to meet the Director of Health Services of Punjab to set things straight. On meeting the director, Dr. Singh brought to her notice the shortcomings of the regulations in providing treatment to drug addiction patients and put forth specific suggestions on treatment through telepsychiatry when the psychiatrist is not physically present at the center while on short leave. However, the reaction of the director was not encouraging as she expressed her helplessness to offer any relaxation in the modality of treatment. She, instead, suggested Dr. Rajinder Singh take up the matter with either the Health Minister or Chief Minister to bring about a change in the existing policy that mandates the physical presence of a psychiatrist while examining patients with drug addiction and dispensing medicines to them. The director turned a deaf ear to Dr. Rajinder Singh's submission to utilize telepsychiatry in case the psychiatrist cannot be physically present at the center owing to certain exigencies.

On 3 June 2023, Dr. Rajinder Singh visited the Health Minister of Punjab to apprise him of the deficiencies in the health policy that rob the patients' right to have treatment. The Health Minister gave a patient hearing to the suggestions offered by Dr. Singh and assured him of rectifying the guidelines that hamper the treatment of patients. The minister was kind enough to ask Dr. Rajinder Singh to be present at the meeting to be held in the middle of June and offer his constructive suggestions to be incorporated into the new policy to be formulated for the benefit of patients.

Dr. Rajinder Singh offered his full obedience to the minister in the larger public interest. The minister also instantly directed the district authorities not to cause harassment to the personnel working at the Akal Drug De-Addiction Centre at Cheema by issuing unwarranted letters. The minister knew that this center was rendering authentic service to society.

The minister understood the situation and how important it is to admit patients with drug addiction who could be at potential risk of attempting suicide, causing harm to themselves and their families, or indulging in criminal activities if denied treatment.

The acknowledgment and appreciation from the Health Minister highlight the exceptional nature of the Akal Drug De-Addiction Centre and Dr. Rajinder Singh's invaluable contribution to society. Despite the prevalence of unethical practices in many other centers, his dedication to preventing drug abuse and treating addiction has stood out.

Since his retirement from the Indian armed forces in 1991, Dr. Rajinder Singh's holistic approach to treatment has benefited approximately 11,000 families affected by substance use disorders. His pledge to provide comprehensive care and support highlights his impact on individuals and communities grappling with addiction-related challenges.

Dr. Rajinder Singh's life is evidence of the impact of simplicity, positivity, and resolute dedication to spiritual and ethical values. His efforts exemplify a lifetime of service marked by his relentless commitment to addressing complex issues and driving positive change. Despite his age, his passion remains undiminished, reflecting his enduring dedication and zeal.

Known for his soft-spoken demeanor and polite nature, Dr. Rajinder Singh is deeply passionate about human welfare, social service, and the evolution of society. His adherence to Guru Nanak's philosophy, which emphasizes serving humanity as a means of serving the divine, highlights his dedication to *seva* (selfless service) and volunteering, particularly for the less privileged and underserved.

As a staunch follower of Sikh principles, he embodies the belief that all beings are interconnected, and fostering harmony and peace among them is essential. His life serves as an inspiring example of how one individual's vow to spiritual values and service can greatly impact society for the better.

Dr. Rajinder Singh's achievements in organizing record-breaking events highlight his innovative and determined approach to addressing societal challenges. These events stand as proof of his staunch commitment to the cause and his ability to mobilize large numbers of people for a common purpose. Through his work, he has set a high standard for advocacy and awareness campaigns, inspiring others to join him in making a positive impact on society.

Massive awareness campaigns, record-breaking rallies, webinars, and symbolic initiatives initiated by him have brought together millions of individuals in the fight against drug abuse. His legacy serves as a powerful reminder of the impact of awareness and collective action in addressing critical mental health care issues and eradicating stigma, ultimately fostering a compassionate and inclusive society.

Dr. Rajinder Singh's initiative under The Kalgidhar Trust has received worldwide appreciation for its unprecedented work on drug awareness. The 'Race Against Drugs' marathon flagged off by the legendary athlete Milkha Singh and the record-breaking walkathon held by students of Akal Academies are just a few examples of the impactful events organized under his leadership. These events, which attracted participation from people of all ages and backgrounds, reflected his resolution to break down barriers and foster community responsibility in the fight against drug addiction.

Bibi Maan Kaur, at 105 years young, a notable figure in her own right, flagged off a marathon for a 'Drug-Free Society' on November 11, 2018, in Chandigarh. Her participation symbolized the spirit needed to combat drug abuse and promote a healthier society.

Additionally, The Kalgidhar Trust achieved another milestone by bagging the World Book of Records (London) award for organizing the largest webinar on June 26, 2020, in observance of the International Day Against Drug Abuse and Illicit Trafficking.

This webinar served as a platform to educate and raise awareness about the dangers of drug abuse, uniting individuals from diverse backgrounds in the global effort to combat this pressing issue.

Dr. Singh's solid resolve to spread awareness about drug abuse transcended physical gatherings, extending to leveraging technology to reach an even wider audience. This innovative approach resulted in setting two world records in the World Book of Records, London.

One of these records was achieved through the organization of the largest webinar on drug abuse, attracting a staggering 80,000 participants. This webinar provided a platform for experts to share insights, knowledge, and solutions related to drug addiction, reaching thousands of individuals eager to learn and contribute to the cause. He further states, "That by creating awareness about the drugs you can reduce and prevent the single greatest cause of mortality and morbidity in the world."

In addition to the webinar, Dr. Rajinder Singh initiated a unique and impactful campaign that generated lakh hand impressions against drug abuse in a single day. This rare event has been registered in the World Book of Records, London. This symbolic gesture encouraged individuals to pledge their faithfulness to fighting drug addiction and supporting those in need. The scale of this campaign illustrated the collective strength of a society united against the scourge of drug abuse.

Dr. Rajinder Singh, a celebrated senior psychiatrist, has garnered a long list of awards, recognitions, and honors throughout his illustrious career. Among these accolades, he was honored with the Award of Human Glory by the SASIIT & R, Mohali, and received the Lifetime Achievement Award from Grey Shades on

July 14, 2023. This award recognized his exceptional contributions and services in the field of drug de-addiction.

Additionally, he has been honored with the Contributors Award by the Current Medical Journal of India and the Award of Excellence by the Indian Medical Association (IMA), Chandigarh, among others. He holds life fellowships with the Indian Psychiatric Society, the Indian Psychiatrist Society (North Zone), the Indian Association for Social Psychiatry, and the Indian Association of Private Psychiatry of India, further underscoring his esteemed status within his profession.

His contribution to addressing drug addiction extends beyond his clinical work to include the publication of two impactful books: 'Drug Addiction' and 'Be Aware, Beware of Drugs'.

His first book, Drug Addiction, delves into the epidemiology and etiology of drug abuse while exploring its devastating health and social consequences. Written with vivid experiences, it serves as a valuable resource for a wide range of readers, including the public, social workers, counselors, psychologists, medical students, family physicians, and NGOs working in the field of drug abuse. It goes beyond merely overcoming addiction to delve into deeper issues of fear, self-awareness, and decision-making.

The second book, Be Aware and Beware of Drugs, was released on the International Day Against Drug Abuse and Illicit Trafficking on June 26, 2022. This book focuses specifically on raising awareness about the harms of various drugs and preventing substance abuse. It has been published in multiple languages, including English, Punjabi, and Hindi, emphasizing the importance of prevention over cure. Dr. Rajinder Singh emphasizes the role of spirituality in filling the void that addicts often try to fill with drugs or alcohol, highlighting the holistic approach taken at the de-addiction centers under his guidance.

Both books have been widely distributed, finding their way into the libraries of approximately 150 schools and 18 universities in Punjab and Himachal Pradesh. They serve as invaluable resources for disseminating knowledge and understanding about the dangers of substance abuse and its societal impact.

Additionally his third book, '"Gems of Wisdom"' is a trove of timeless words of inspiration and wisdom of the great philosophers, thinkers, and intellectuals of the world.

Dr. Singh's efforts to eradicate the social stigma associated with psychiatric disorders and drug addiction have been truly commendable. Through massive awareness campaigns, seminars, and talks organized in universities, colleges, and schools across Punjab, Chandigarh, and Himachal Pradesh, he has played a crucial role in challenging deeply ingrained social stigmas.

By educating millions of people, especially children and youth, about the harms of drugs and the importance of seeking help for mental health issues, he has reshaped perceptions and fostered greater acceptance and empathy toward those struggling with these challenges. His initiatives have not only transformed public perception but have also inspired a sense of community responsibility, encouraging people from all walks of life to join the fight against drug abuse.

Through his relentless pursuit of awareness and education, Dr. Rajinder Singh continues to make an impact in breaking down barriers and promoting a culture of understanding and support for individuals facing psychiatric disorders and addiction.

Dr. Singh's groundbreaking research signifies his pioneering spirit and innovative approach to healthcare. His study titled The Long-Term Impact of a Holistic Inpatient Treatment Program for Substance Use Disorders: 498 Patients Personally Revisited after 5-10 Years stands as the world's first-ever examination of its kind. Conducted at a rural drug de-addiction center, this research provides valuable insights into the long-term effectiveness of holistic treatment methods that integrate spirituality with traditional approaches to managing drug addiction.

Published in the esteemed Indian Journal of Social Psychiatry in 2023, Dr. Rajinder Singh's study represents a significant contribution to the global healthcare community. By personally revisiting 498 patients after 5-10 years, he offers empirical evidence of the enduring impact of holistic inpatient treatment programs on substance use disorders. He sincerely acknowledges the help and contribution of Dr. SS Advani, a resolute volunteer from Mumbai, in this research work and various drug awareness programs in Punjab and Himachal Pradesh.

This research not only solidifies Dr. Singh's reputation as an innovator in the field but also underlines his resolve to advance knowledge and understanding in addiction management. By including spirituality with conventional medical practices, his study opens new avenues for holistic approaches to drug addiction treatment, ultimately benefiting patients worldwide.

His influence on mental health education and awareness in India is intense and far-reaching. Beyond his direct involvement in patient care and research, he has played a pivotal role in training thousands of nursing and public health students, educators, and healthcare practitioners. Through his efforts, these individuals are equipped with the knowledge and skills to identify and diagnose early signs of mental health issues, thereby enabling timely intervention and support.

Furthermore, his contributions have been instrumental in the prevention of drug addiction and suicides. By raising awareness about the risks associated with substance abuse and promoting mental well-being, he has helped communities across India address these pressing public health concerns. Through his tireless advocacy and educational initiatives, he continues to make a significant impact on mental health outcomes and the overall well-being of individuals and communities.

Conclusion

A Generous Soul

In the corridors of history, amidst the vast expanse of human achievements, there are rare souls who go beyond the boundaries of their own existence to become guiding stars for humanity. At the core of Dr. Rajinder Singh's being resided a sense of generosity, a quality that surpassed material wealth or worldly recognition. His generosity wasn't merely in the form of monetary donations or grand gestures; rather, it emanated from his very essence, reflected in his actions, thoughts, and words.

One of the most noteworthy aspects of Dr. Singh's generosity was his dedication to education. He believed that knowledge was the greatest gift one could imbibe and impart, and he dedicated his life to sharing this gift with the world. Despite his towering intellect and numerous accomplishments, Dr. Rajinder Singh remained humble and approachable, always willing to engage with youngsters and aspiring doctors and researchers. His interactions with youngsters weren't just moments of imparting; they were opportunities to bring them back onto the right path and inspire the next generation of innovators.

His generosity extended beyond the boundaries of his own career. He is a global citizen, advocating for welfare among the youth of India. In a world often divided by politics and ideology, he championed the cause of humanity, emphasizing the importance of collaboration in tackling the challenges that surpass borders. His vision for a better world wasn't confined to lofty conversations about him; it was grounded in the simple yet strong belief that kindness and compassion could bridge even the widest chasms of differences.

In a world often characterized by self-interest and competition, Dr. Singh's generosity stood as a demonstration of the power of empathy and altruism. He understood that true greatness lay not in personal achievements or accolades but in the ability to uplift others and make a positive difference in their lives. His legacy isn't just measured in terms of breakthroughs or accomplishments; it lives on in the countless lives he touched with his kindness, wisdom, and boundless generosity.

At the heart of his work lies ambition, a relentless drive to push boundaries and achieve greatness. His insatiable thirst for knowledge and desire to shape the world through medicine propelled him to the forefront of the revolution. It came from the great values he learned and imbibed from his parents, brother, and teachers. He took matters into his own hands when it was much needed and walked on the path of change. A little step and then some more, just for the young generation and their future. He never stood back. Many times, adversities hold us back, but it did the opposite for him. He pushed the doors to his limit and opened limitless opportunities for himself and others to create a future that was bigger than what those kids wanted for themselves. When life threw difficulties in his way, he didn't fall back; he dealt with the problems. He always believed in the bigger picture and the purpose God wanted for him. Till today, he is living his life for the betterment of others, keeping his values in his head and heart. He believes his purpose in life is to impart values and goodness and share them with other human beings.

As we reflect on the life and legacy of Dr. Rajinder Singh, let us remember him not only as a brilliant doctor or a visionary leader but as a generous soul who illuminated the world with his warmth, compassion, and humanity. Let us strive to embody his spirit of generosity in our own lives, knowing that in doing so, we honor not just his memory but the very essence of what it means to be truly human.

His life from humble beginnings serves as a poignant reminder of the power of perseverance and purpose. Born into a modest family in a small village, his early life was marked by simplicity and scarcity. His parents instilled in him the values of hard work, integrity, and humility. Despite facing financial constraints, his thirst for knowledge knew no bounds. He walked miles to attend school and college, his fortitude fueled by the belief that education was the key to a brighter future. From those humble beginnings emerged a giant of science and a light of hope for millions around the world.

Retrying, not retired, is a fitting description of this 91-year-old, who is relentlessly working to save the 19-year-olds from the clutches of drugs.

THE COLONEL'S JOURNAL

The Colonel's Journal

WHY DRUGS?

The Power of Spiritual Therapy in Holistic Healing for Drug Addiction

Dr. (Col.) Rajinder Singh

Former Senior Advisor, Psychiatry, Armed Forces

February 26, 2024

In the realm of behavioral health, treating drug addiction requires a multifaceted approach that goes beyond traditional methods. One powerful yet often underutilized tool is spiritual therapy. As a psychiatrist, I have witnessed firsthand the profound impact it can have on patients' journeys to recovery. Here are some key points to consider when incorporating spiritual therapy, particularly through practices like daily prayers and meditation, into your treatment approach:

1. **Cultivating Inner Peace**: Drug addiction often stems from a deep sense of inner turmoil. Spiritual therapy, including meditation and prayer, helps individuals cultivate inner peace. These practices teach patients to quiet their minds, find solace

in the present moment, and develop a sense of calm amidst life's challenges.

2. **Building Spiritual Strength**: Drug addiction can leave individuals feeling spiritually bankrupt. Spiritual therapy offers a path to rebuild that strength. By connecting with their spiritual beliefs, patients can rediscover a sense of purpose and meaning, which can serve as a powerful motivator in their recovery journey.

3. **Building Connection**: Drug addiction can be isolating, leading to feelings of loneliness and disconnection. Spiritual practices often emphasize community and connection, providing patients with a sense of belonging and support. Group prayer or meditation sessions can be particularly impactful in this regard.

4. **Promoting Mindfulness**: Mindfulness is a key component of many spiritual practices. By teaching patients to be more present and aware of their thoughts and feelings, spiritual therapy helps them better understand the underlying causes of their drug addiction and develop healthier coping mechanisms. Let us embrace the past with gusto, the present with mindfulness, and the future with hope.

5. **Providing Guidance**: Spiritual beliefs can offer a moral compass for individuals struggling with drug addiction. Spiritual therapy provides patients with a framework for making positive choices and navigating challenges in their recovery journey.

6. **Relapse Prevention**: Most importantly, spiritual therapy can be a powerful tool in preventing relapse. By helping patients develop a strong sense of self and a deep connection

to something greater, spiritual practices provide the resilience needed to resist the temptation of drugs.

In conclusion, incorporating spiritual therapy, such as daily prayers and meditation, into drug addiction treatment can offer great benefits. It helps patients find inner peace, build spiritual strength and connection, promote mindfulness, and provide guidance. These effects empower patients with the stability, firmness, and strength to combat feelings of powerlessness, vulnerability, and helplessness. By integrating spiritual therapy into holistic healing approaches, behavioral health workers can provide a more comprehensive and effective path to recovery, aiding patients in overcoming drug addiction and finding lasting peace and fulfillment.

***

10 Rare Facts About Smoking

Dr. (Col.) Rajinder Singh

Former Senior Advisor, Psychiatry, Armed Forces

November 20, 2023

1. **Chemical Onslaught with Every Puff**: Inhaling tobacco smoke introduces a staggering 7,000 chemicals, many of which are highly toxic and carcinogenic, with each puff.

2. **Genetic Impact Beyond the Lungs**: Smoking not only damages the DNA in lung cells but also extends its impact to other tissues throughout the body. This reveals the acute systemic influence of smoking on our genetic material.

3. **Devastating Toll on Global Health**: Tobacco is the leading cause of 73% of drug-related deaths worldwide annually. A

chilling statistic shows that 8.7 million lives are claimed by tobacco out of the 11.9 million drug-related deaths each year.

4. **Brain Under Oxidative Stress**: Smoking contributes to oxidative stress in the brain, a factor implicated in the development of neurodegenerative diseases. Ongoing research explores links between smoking and conditions like Alzheimer's disease.

5. **Fragile Foundations: Smoking and Bone Health**: Linked to decreased bone density and an elevated risk of fractures, smoking poses a particular threat to postmenopausal women by accelerating bone loss and contributing to osteoporosis.

6. **Fertility's Silent Struggle**: Smoking silently affects fertility, diminishing sperm count and motility in men while disrupting reproductive hormones in women, reducing the chances of successful conception.

7. **Skin's Premature Aging Journey**: The aging process of the skin accelerates under the influence of smoking. Premature wrinkles, sagging skin, and a lackluster complexion result from the constriction of blood vessels, which reduces oxygen and essential nutrient supply to the skin.

8. **Smoking's Blurred Vision**: Smoking is intricately linked to an elevated risk of age-related macular degeneration (AMD), a leading cause of vision loss in older adults. Smokers face a higher likelihood of developing AMD compared to non-smokers.

9. **Second-hand Smoke's Unseen Threat**: Exposure to second-hand smoke increases the risk of Sudden Infant Death

Syndrome (SIDS) in infants. Babies exposed to smoke before and after birth face a higher risk of this tragic syndrome.

10. **Hidden Strain on the Heart's Harmony**: Beyond its known impact on heart health, smoking also affects the smaller blood vessels around the heart. This hidden influence disrupts the smooth flow of blood to the heart muscle, even without major blockages in the main arteries. It's like a subtle discord in the cardiovascular system caused by tobacco smoke.

These hidden truths underscore the diverse and extensive impacts of smoking on health, emphasizing the urgent need for smoking cessation for the sake of overall well-being.

***

Unplugging the Mind: Understanding and Managing Digital Addiction

Dr. (Col.) Rajinder Singh

Former Senior Advisor, Psychiatry, Armed Forces

November 10, 2023

Introduction

In the age of smartphones, social media, and constant connectivity, addiction is no longer limited to substances like drugs and alcohol— it now extends to the digital world. As a psychiatrist, I have witnessed the rising tide of digital addiction and its impact on mental health and well-being. In this blog, I explore digital addiction from a psychiatric perspective, delving into its causes, consequences, and strategies for prevention and treatment.

Defining Digital Addiction

Digital addiction, also referred to as internet addiction or technology addiction, is a behavioral addiction characterized by excessive and compulsive use of digital devices, the internet, and online services. While it does not involve substances, it shares similarities with traditional addictions, such as withdrawal symptoms, tolerance, and impaired control over usage.

Causes and Risk Factors

1. **Escapism**: Many individuals turn to the digital world as a way to escape challenges and stressors in real life. The instant gratification and distractions offered by digital devices can be highly appealing.

2. **Dopamine Release**: Social media, gaming, and other online platforms are designed to trigger the release of dopamine in the brain, creating pleasurable sensations. Over time, this reinforcement can lead to addictive behaviors.

3. **FOMO (Fear of Missing Out)**: The fear of missing out on social events, news, or updates drives individuals to stay constantly connected, leading to an obsession with checking notifications and feeds.

4. **Other Factors**: Feelings of loneliness, isolation, lack of social and family support, work-related stress, and low self-esteem can all increase the risk of digital addiction.

5. **Accessibility**: The integration of digital devices into daily life makes it easy for people to fall into a routine of constant use.

Consequences of Digital Addiction

1. **Mental Health Impacts**: Digital addiction has been linked to anxiety, depression, and low self-esteem. Constant comparison to others on social media can fuel feelings of inadequacy and loneliness.

2. **Physical Health Problems**: Prolonged screen time can result in issues such as eye strain, disrupted sleep patterns, and musculoskeletal problems.

3. **Impaired Social Relationships**: Excessive use of digital devices can hinder face-to-face social interactions, leading to strained relationships and isolation.

4. **Decreased Productivity**: The constant need to check emails, social media, or apps can lead to decreased productivity and increased work-related stress.

5. **Neglect of Responsibilities**: Constant preoccupation with the internet can lead to neglect of work, school, or household duties, as maximum time is spent on social media.

6. **Financial Consequences**: In-app purchases, online gambling, and subscription services can strain finances, resulting in financial difficulties.

Prevention and Treatment

Preventing and addressing digital addiction is crucial for maintaining a healthy balance between the virtual and real worlds. Dr. Singh suggests the following strategies:

1. **Digital Detox**: Periodically disconnect from digital devices and engage in offline activities. Start with short breaks and gradually extend them.

2. **Set Boundaries**: Establish clear rules for device usage, both personally and for family members. Limit screen time, particularly during meals and before bedtime.

3. **Seek Professional Help**: If digital addiction is interfering with daily life, consider seeking help from a mental health professional, such as a psychiatrist or counselor.

4. **Mindfulness and Stress Management**: Learning stress management techniques and practicing mindfulness can help cope with anxiety and other emotional challenges that may lead to digital addiction.

5. **Support Groups**: Joining support groups or online communities focused on digital addiction can provide valuable insights and encouragement.

Conclusion

Digital addiction is a growing concern in today's hyper-connected world. I urge individuals to be mindful of their digital habits and the impact these habits have on mental and emotional well-being. Recognizing the signs of digital addiction and taking proactive steps to manage it can lead to a healthier, more balanced life. By striking a balance between the digital and real worlds, we can mitigate the negative consequences of digital addiction and promote overall mental health and well-being.

***

Ravi Arora's Fight for Sobriety: Battling Addiction Triggered by Kidney Stone Medication

Dr. (Col.) Rajinder Singh

Former Senior Advisor, Psychiatry, Armed Forces

November 10, 2023

In the heart of Tarn Taran, Ravi Arora, a 44-year-old pharmacist with 13 years of experience in his chemist shop, was ensnared in the darkness of addiction. His path to recovery and transformation began at the Akal Drug De-Addiction Centre.

Ravi's descent into addiction started in 2007 when he was prescribed Fortwin injections for kidney stone pain. These medically necessary injections soon became a source of pleasure, and Ravi fell into a relentless daily cycle of consuming 1 ml injections. His family uncovered the truth when they noticed injection scars, prompting grave concern.

Married, having a young son, Ravi lived with his parents amidst strained familial ties, partly due to business disputes. The ready availability of drugs, facilitated by a compounding chemist, beckoned him back into addiction after five to six years of sobriety. His relapse coincided with the birth of his second son.

In an effort to rebuild his life, Ravi reopened his chemist shop with the support of his in-laws, but the accessibility of opium dwindled during the lockdown. Turning to Alprax 0.5 and Tramadol 100 mg, he hoped to stay active during the day. It was a wake-up call from his elder son, aspiring to clear the NEET exam or migrate to Canada, that drove him to seek help.

Determined to heal, Ravi returned to the Akal Drug De-Addiction Centre, where he had sought assistance over a decade ago. Since his return in early May, he has diligently followed the prescribed treatment regimen, finding a semblance of normalcy. His cravings have subsided, allowing him to rest peacefully at night.

With a clear goal in mind, Ravi is resolute about reuniting with his son in Canada. He is committed to continuing treatment, recognizing that the path to full recovery may take five to eight years. The spiritual ambiance at the center helps him stay focused and avoid slipping back into old habits.

Ravi Arora's story is a powerful example of the human capacity for redemption. It underscores the importance of determination and highlights the critical role that institutions like the Akal Drug De-Addiction Centre play in empowering individuals to reclaim their lives and pursue their most cherished dreams.

***

Unveiling the Horrors of Heroin: Journey into Its Chilling Composition

Dr. (Col.) Rajinder Singh

Former Senior Advisor, Psychiatry, Armed Forces

August 16, 2023

In a world filled with challenges, the allure of escape can be tempting. Yet, hidden within this escape is a treacherous path paved with the sinister components of heroin. As a psychiatrist, I have witnessed the devastating impact of this substance firsthand. In this discussion, I unveil the harsh realities of addiction, shedding light on the dreadful constituents of heroin and the destruction it brings.

Morphine Infusion: An Illusory Embrace

Heroin offers a fleeting sense of euphoria, coupled with a numbing of pain. Once in the body, it swiftly metabolizes into morphine, initiating the first step in its seductive pull. This illusory embrace tightens its grip over time, leading the unsuspecting user into the clutches of addiction.

Amplifying Agents: Acetyl's Stealthy Hold

Behind the scenes, acetyl groups act as amplifiers, enhancing heroin's potency. These seemingly harmless molecules facilitate its swift journey into the brain, intensifying its effects on the central nervous system. This dangerous dance complicates the battle for control over the mind.

Synthetic Intruders: Concealed Dangers

As I delved deeper, I discovered the most disturbing truth: heroin's makeup extends beyond morphine and acetyl groups. Synthetic additives like fentanyl, often introduced without the user's knowledge, add a lethal twist to the equation. These additives can elevate heroin's potency to life-threatening levels, pushing users to the edge.

Uncertainty Lurks: A Game of Roulette

Street heroin often hides another deadly secret—unknown contaminants. With every dose, users gamble with their lives, potentially injecting hazardous impurities that drastically increase the risks to their health and safety.

Toxic Residues: Lingering Poison

Heroin's production leaves behind a grim residue—a toxic legacy of chemicals and solvents. This corrosive mixture attacks the body, slowly eroding vitality and health and leaving behind devastation in its wake.

Reaping Destruction: Malevolent Aftermath

The consequences of heroin use are catastrophic. Collapsed veins, damaged organs, and the constant threat of infections like HIV and Hepatitis C paint a harrowing picture. What began as a temporary escape transforms into an unending cycle of pain and destruction, a cost far too great for a fleeting moment of relief.

Choose Life: Breaking the Chains

As I uncover the harrowing components that define heroin, one message becomes clear: the choice lies in our hands. Amidst the darkness of addiction, there is always a glimmer of hope. It is the decision to break free from the chains of addiction, seek help, and embrace a life free from the shackles of substances.

Though the road to recovery may be challenging, it offers a path toward liberation, strength, and renewal. It is a journey toward light, away from the chilling composition of heroin. In the end, the power to choose life remains with each individual—an opportunity to break free from the nightmare of addiction.

***

Global Cannabis Dependence: Unveiling the 4% Struggle

Dr. (Col.) Rajinder Singh

Former Senior Advisor, Psychiatry, Armed Forces

I highlight ten potential harms that cannabis could have on youth aged 15-16 years, noting that 4% of the global population is struggling with cannabis dependence:

- **Cognitive Impact**: Cannabis use during critical brain development stages may lead to reduced memory and learning abilities.

- **Academic Decline**: Focus and concentration issues stemming from cannabis dependence can result in lower academic performance.

- **Mental Health Risks**: There is an increased likelihood of developing anxiety and depression associated with cannabis dependence.

- **Social Isolation**: Forming healthy social connections may become challenging due to cannabis dependence.

- **Addiction Vulnerability**: Those dependent on cannabis are at a higher risk of developing future substance addictions.

- **Decision-Making Impairment**: Cannabis dependence can compromise judgment and decision-making abilities.

- **Legal Consequences**: Dependence on cannabis might lead to legal issues, particularly for underage users.

- **Physical Health Concerns**: Cannabis use can potentially have negative effects on lung health and overall well-being.

- **Impact on Future Opportunities**: Cannabis dependence could hinder educational and employment prospects.

- **Risk of Substance Abuse**: Individuals struggling with cannabis dependence are more susceptible to trying other substances.

Moreover, the legalization of cannabis in countries like the United States and others has resulted in a concerning increase in cannabis abuse. The availability and societal acceptance of cannabis may contribute to a higher prevalence of dependence issues, particularly among youth. To address these potential harms, I advocate for a comprehensive approach that includes education, prevention, mental health support, and accessible treatment options.

***

From Darkness to Triumph: Navdeep Singh's Inspiring Battle Against Addiction

Dr. (Col.) Rajinder Singh

Former Senior Advisor in Psychiatry, Armed Forces

August 9, 2023

In the transformative journey of Navdeep Singh, the ebb and flow of emotions have shaped his path from darkness to hope and resilience. At the tender age of 22, he found himself ensnared in the clutches of *chitta*, a challenging descent that began in 2019. As the drug tightened its grip around him, Navdeep battled feelings of despair, helplessness, and isolation, unsure if he could ever break free from its chains.

In 2021, he made the courageous decision to seek treatment by admitting himself to a drug de-addiction center near Bhadson, where he endured five painstaking months of therapy. However, life's relentless twists took him down an unexpected path. Approximately four months before his success story, a dark chapter opened, and Navdeep found himself pulled back into the abyss of addiction. A friend's influence led him astray, and once again, the drug took center stage in his life. The pain of his relapse weighed heavily on his heart, filled with remorse for slipping back into addiction's clutches.

Amidst the challenges, Navdeep clung to a flicker of hope—the dream of a better life in the United Kingdom. This aspiration became his beacon, igniting a fire of determination to break free from the clutches of *chitta* once and for all. Fueled by this desire, he mustered the courage to seek solace and salvation at the Akal Drug De-Addiction Centre in Cheema Sahib.

Within the center's confines, Navdeep experienced an absolute transformation. Surrounded by compassionate medical professionals and empathetic support staff, he found a sanctuary of healing and understanding. The center's spiritual ambiance, yoga sessions, and regular physical fitness activities became crucial pillars in his recovery journey, restoring not only his physical health but also nourishing his soul.

In the depths of his soul-searching, Navdeep revealed the emotional wounds that had led him astray. Love lost and the sting of rejection left scars intertwined with his addiction. Yet, amidst his struggles, he found the strength to reach out to his current girlfriend, who was also trapped in the same nightmarish cycle. His determination to help her break free resonated with a blend of vulnerability and courage.

Throughout his journey, Navdeep faced the grim consequences of drug addiction, bearing the burden of contracting hepatitis—a stark reminder of the reckless choices that had once defined his life. These scars etched a poignant story of pain, regret, and a burning desire to rewrite his narrative.

Driven by a deep sense of responsibility, Navdeep emerged as a passionate advocate for change. His voice rang loud and clear, demanding stricter measures against the rampant sale of *chitta* that plagued the society he once knew. The insidious nexus between politicians, police, and drug peddlers became a target for his passionate plea for justice.

As he embarks on his dream of going to the United Kingdom, Navdeep stands as a testament to the human spirit's resilience. The journey has not been easy, and the shadows of addiction have cast long, dark stretches in his past. However, through the support of his loving family and the light of hope provided by the de-addiction center, he now stands tall as an inspiring success story—a living testament to courage, transformation, and the power of healing.

***

Unveiling the Truth: 9 Startling Facts About Tobacco

Dr. (Col.) Rajinder Singh

Former Senior Advisor in Psychiatry, Armed Forces

July 29, 2023

Tobacco, a plant cultivated for centuries, is widely used in various forms, including cigarettes, cigars, and smokeless tobacco products. While its cultural significance may be rooted in history, its impact on public health is far from benign. Today, we'll delve into the dark side of tobacco and explore nine shocking facts that shed light on its harmful effects.

1. **Highly Addictive and Toxic Substance**: At the core of tobacco's allure lies nicotine, a highly addictive and toxic substance. Once inhaled or ingested, nicotine rapidly reaches the brain, triggering the release of dopamine and leading to addiction. Breaking free from this addiction can be an arduous journey, as withdrawal symptoms can be both physically and mentally challenging.

2. **7,000 Chemicals in a Single Puff**: It's alarming to discover that a single puff of tobacco smoke contains around 7,000 chemicals. These chemicals include numerous harmful substances, many of which are carcinogenic, meaning they have the potential to cause cancer. This revelation underscores the dangers of even casual tobacco use.

3. **A Toxic Cocktail**: Besides nicotine, tobacco contains a toxic cocktail of chemicals. Notable culprits include tar, carbon monoxide, nitrogen oxide, hydrogen cyanide, vinyl chloride, radioactive compounds, metals, and benzene. Each of these compounds poses significant threats to the body, increasing the risks of various diseases.

4. **Global Impact on Lives**: The devastating impact of tobacco claims a staggering 8.7 million lives worldwide every year. This shocking statistic should serve as a wake-up call to the global community, urging collective efforts to combat tobacco-related illnesses.

5. **India's Grim Reality**: In India alone, approximately 1.2 million people lose their lives annually due to tobacco-related health hazards. This highlights the urgent need for comprehensive tobacco control measures and public awareness campaigns to save lives and protect the nation's health.

6. **A Leading Cause of Cancer**: Cancer, a group of diseases characterized by uncontrollable cell growth, claims countless lives each year. Alarmingly, about 40% of all cancer cases can be linked to tobacco consumption. This correlation underscores the critical importance of prevention and cessation efforts.

7. **Impact on Cardiovascular Health**: Tobacco use doesn't merely target the lungs; it also takes a toll on cardiovascular health. Smoking raises blood pressure and heart rate, making users more susceptible to heart disease, strokes, and other cardiovascular disorders.

8. **A Global Menace**: Tobacco ranks as the leading cause of mortality and morbidity worldwide. This pervasive issue affects not only individual users but also communities and healthcare systems on a global scale.

9. **Preventable Cause of Death**: Perhaps the most heart-wrenching fact is that tobacco-related deaths are largely preventable. By increasing awareness, promoting smoking cessation programs, and implementing effective tobacco control policies, we can save millions of lives and create a healthier future for generations to come. Global Adult Tobacco Survey (GATS 2017) reveals a 6% decrease in Tobacco use in India due to anti-tobacco efforts (WHO, 2017).

Conclusion:

The journey to combat the detrimental effects of tobacco may be an uphill battle, but armed with knowledge, awareness, and collective determination, we can make a significant impact. Each person who chooses to quit or never starts using tobacco contributes to a healthier world. Let's spread the word about the truth of tobacco and work together to build a future free from its grasp.

***

5 Symptoms to Notice Whether Your Child is Slipping into Drug Abuse: By Dr. Rajinder Singh (Awarded Psychiatrist)

Dr. (Col.) Rajinder Singh

Former Senior Advisor, Psychiatry, Armed Forces

July 27, 2023

As parents, ensuring the well-being of our children is paramount. Unfortunately, drug abuse among adolescents is a growing concern in today's society. Recognizing the signs of drug abuse in your child is crucial for early intervention and providing the necessary support. Here are five symptoms to watch for:

1. **Behavioral Changes**: Keep an eye out for significant shifts in your child's behavior. Sudden mood swings, withdrawal from family and friends, increased aggression, or irritability can be red flags. A loss of interest in activities they once enjoyed or dropping out of social circles is also a concerning sign. Changes in behavior often serve as early indicators of potential drug abuse.

2. **Physical Signs**: Watch for any unusual physical changes in your child. These may include sudden weight loss, bloodshot or watery eyes, frequent nosebleeds, or trembling hands. Physical symptoms like these could indicate drug misuse or abuse. Pay attention to persistent changes and address them promptly.

3. **Academic or Work Decline**: Monitor your child's academic or work performance closely. A sudden drop in grades, frequent absenteeism, or a loss of interest in school or work-related activities might be linked to drug use. Declines in academic or work performance can result from the distraction and negative impact of drug abuse.

4. **Changes in Social Habits**: Notice any shifts in your child's social life. If they start distancing themselves from old friends and forming new, secretive relationships, it could signal involvement in drug-related activities. Changes in social habits, such as spending time with peers who exhibit similar signs, should be taken seriously.

5. **Neglecting Personal Appearance**: Pay attention to your child's personal hygiene and appearance. A sudden lack of interest in grooming, a messy appearance, or unusual smells on their breath or clothes might indicate drug use. Neglecting personal appearance is often associated with a preoccupation with drug abuse.

It's essential to remember that these signs can vary based on individual circumstances, and not all symptoms may be present. Approach the situation with empathy and open communication. If you observe multiple symptoms or suspect drug abuse, consider seeking professional help or counseling to address the issue effectively.

Early intervention can make a significant difference in preventing drug abuse from taking a toll on your child's life. By staying vigilant and fostering a supportive environment, we can help our children make healthy choices and steer clear of the dangers of drug abuse.

***

The Colonel's Journal

The Timeless Mental 'Wealth'

The Spiritual Essence of 'Good Vibes' in Psychiatry

Dr. (Col.) Rajinder Singh

Former Senior Advisor, Psychiatry, Armed Forces

January 22, 2024

Introduction

In the intricate tapestry of psychiatry, the significance of exuding positive energy, characterized by spiritual depth and empathetic resonance, goes beyond just the atmosphere of the office. As a psychiatrist deeply committed to the well-being of my patients, I aim to explore the transformative power of 'good vibes' that stem from a deep sense of spirituality and heightened empathy.

Understanding 'Good Vibes' in Psychiatry

In the sacred space of psychiatry, 'good vibes' extend beyond the physical confines of an office, reaching into the spiritual core of the psychiatrist. This concept involves cultivating empathy, compassion, and a genuine connection that goes beyond the clinical encounter. Such spiritual depth significantly contributes to the therapeutic process and enhances the overall well-being of the patient.

Personal Journey: A Spiritual Awakening

I encountered a transformative experience that emphasized the spiritual essence of 'good vibes' in psychiatry when I met Aryan, a young man battling severe depression. Aryan was engulfed in a sense of spiritual emptiness, searching for solace beyond conventional clinical interventions.

Recognizing the significance of spiritual resonance in healing, I introduced a deeper spiritual approach to their sessions through mindfulness practices, guided meditation, and empathetic listening. The 'good vibes' that emerged from this shared journey became a powerful source of healing for Aryan, leading him toward recovery.

Case Study: Aryan's Spiritual Rebirth

Aryan's case serves as a testament to the transformative impact of spiritual 'good vibes' in psychiatry. By marrying evidence-based interventions with a shared spiritual exploration, Aryan not only found relief from his depressive symptoms but also underwent a profound spiritual rebirth.

Takeaway for Behavioral Health Workers

The lesson from Aryan's story is important for all behavioral health workers: The energy we emanate as psychiatrists goes beyond clinical knowledge; it involves tapping into our spiritual reservoir and fostering connections that transcend the material world. Recognizing the spiritual essence of 'good vibes' means co-creating a healing space where the patient's spirit is acknowledged and nurtured.

Conclusion

As behavioral health workers, let us embrace the transformative power of spirituality within our practice. By radiating 'good vibes' grounded in empathy and spiritual depth, we can impact those seeking our guidance. In this sacred dance of psychiatry, the spiritual energy we bring becomes a guiding light for patients on their journey toward mental and spiritual well-being.

***

Beyond Prescriptions: A Journey of Empathy and Healing

Dr. (Col.) Rajinder Singh

Former Senior Advisor, Psychiatry, Armed Forces

January 15, 2024

In the serene city of Chandigarh, my 56-year career as a psychiatrist has been defined by a commitment to compassionate care. One particularly poignant chapter unfolded with Prerna, a 28-year-old woman grappling with persistent chest pain that had evaded diagnosis from various specialists.

Prerna's journey through countless medical consultations left her frustrated and despondent until a compassionate psychologist recognized the depth of her distress and referred her to me.

As I delved into Prerna's story, I uncovered layers of stress deeply intertwined with her personal life. Rather than resorting to prescriptions, I spent months simply listening—an art I had honed over decades. Gradually, Prerna began to open up, revealing the intricacies of her struggles.

Her story was important: As the primary caregiver for her paralyzed mother, Prerna faced immense societal pressure to remarry. Yet, her heart was devoted to being an unwavering support for her ailing mother. In a world driven by quick fixes, my approach was grounded in empathetic listening, free from self-promotion or financial gain.

Over the course of our sessions, Prerna underwent a powerful transformation. Healing emerged not through medication, but through the genuine care and understanding I provided. With my guidance, Prerna found a resolution that aligned with her deepest convictions, anchored in her love and sense of duty.

Moral of the Story

This narrative underscores a simple yet great truth: empathy and compassion unburdened by self-promotion possess unparalleled potency. Prerna's story is a testament to the healing potential that arises when a behavioral health specialist prioritizes understanding over prescriptions. In the realm of mental health, the gift of genuine listening becomes a therapeutic intervention—an invaluable testament to its transformative power.

***

Navigating the Crossroads: Mental Health and Menopause

Dr. (Col.) Rajinder Singh

Former Senior Advisor, Psychiatry, Armed Forces

January 4, 2024

Menopause, a natural transition in a woman's life, is often associated with physical changes such as hot flashes and night sweats. However, beyond these visible symptoms lies a complex interplay between hormonal shifts and mental health. Understanding this link is crucial for women navigating this transformative stage and for those who support them.

The Hormonal Rollercoaster

During menopause, the key female hormones—estrogen and progesterone—undergo a dramatic decline. These hormonal fluctuations can significantly impact the production of neurotransmitters, the brain's chemical messengers responsible for mood, sleep, and overall well-being. This change can lead to a range of mental health challenges, including:

1. **Mood Swings and Irritability:** Estrogen fluctuations can cause sudden shifts in mood, leading to feelings of anxiety and increased irritability.

2. **Depression and Anxiety:** Studies suggest a higher prevalence of depression and anxiety during perimenopause and menopause. This may be linked to hormonal changes as well as other life stressors.

3. **Sleep Disturbances:** A drop in estrogen can disrupt sleep patterns, resulting in insomnia, fatigue, and daytime drowsiness.

4. **Brain Fog and Cognitive Decline:** Some women report difficulties in concentration, forgetfulness, and reduced cognitive function during this period.

Breaking the Silence

Despite the prevalence of mental health challenges during menopause, many women remain silent. They may attribute these changes to the natural aging process or feel embarrassed to seek help. This silence can exacerbate existing symptoms and hinder overall quality of life.

Empowering Change

The good news is that there are effective strategies to manage the impact of menopause on mental health:

1. **Healthy Lifestyle:** Maintaining a balanced diet, engaging in regular exercise, and ensuring adequate sleep can significantly enhance well-being and help regulate mood.

2. **Mindfulness and Relaxation Techniques:** Practices like meditation, yoga, and deep breathing can effectively manage stress and promote relaxation, reducing anxiety and improving mood.

3. **Social Support:** Building a strong support network of friends, family, and support groups can provide essential emotional support and guidance during this transition.

4. **Seeking Professional Help:** Don't hesitate to reach out to a therapist or counselor who can offer specialized support and treatment for mental health challenges during menopause.

5. **Hormone Replacement Therapy:** In some cases, hormone replacement therapy can alleviate mood swings and other symptoms. However, it's vital to discuss this option thoroughly with a healthcare professional.

Beyond the Physical

Menopause represents more than just a physical transition; it encompasses emotional and mental changes as well. Recognizing the link between hormonal fluctuations and mental health is crucial for women to navigate this crossroad confidently and seek support when needed. Remember, you are not alone in this journey. By prioritizing your mental well-being alongside your physical health, you can embrace menopause as a positive chapter in your life.

***

Nutrition for Mental Wellness: A Holistic Approach

Dr. (Col.) Rajinder Singh

Former Senior Advisor, Psychiatry, Armed Forces

December 12, 2023

Introduction

The food we eat significantly influences our overall health and well-being, including our mental health. While a single meal won't magically cure a mental health condition, making consistent, healthy dietary choices can positively impact our mood, energy levels, and cognitive function over time.

How Food Affects Mental Health

There are several ways in which our dietary choices can affect mental health:

1. **Nutrient Deficiencies:** Deficiencies in key nutrients such as vitamin B12, omega-3 fatty acids, and vitamin D are linked to an increased risk of mental health conditions like depression and anxiety.

2. **Gut Health:** Often referred to as the 'second brain', the gut plays a vital role in mood and mental well-being. A healthy gut microbiome promotes the production of neurotransmitters like serotonin, essential for regulating mood. Consuming a diet rich in fiber and fermented foods can enhance gut health and improve mental wellness.

3. **Inflammation:** Chronic inflammation has been associated with several mental health conditions, including depression and anxiety. Eating a diet rich in fruits, vegetables, and whole grains can help reduce inflammation in the body.

4. **Blood Sugar Levels:** Rapid fluctuations in blood sugar can impact mood and energy. A balanced diet that includes protein, healthy fats, and complex carbohydrates can help stabilize blood sugar levels.

Foods to Promote Mental Well-being

While there is no one-size-fits-all mental health diet, certain foods are known to be beneficial for brain health and mood:

1. **Fruits and Vegetables:** Rich in vitamins, minerals, and antioxidants, fruits and vegetables are essential for brain function and protecting against neurodegenerative diseases.

2. **Whole Grains:** Whole grains provide complex carbohydrates, fiber, and essential nutrients that help stabilize blood sugar levels and deliver sustained energy.

3. **Lean Protein:** Sources like fish, poultry, and legumes are crucial for brain development and function.

4. **Healthy Fats:** Omega-3 fatty acids found in fatty fish like salmon and tuna are vital for brain function and mood regulation.

5. **Fermented Foods:** Foods like yogurt, kimchi, and sauerkraut are rich in probiotics, which promote gut health and can improve mood.

Foods to Limit

While some foods can enhance mental well-being, others may have adverse effects. Here are foods to limit or avoid:

1. **Added Sugar:** This can contribute to inflammation, disrupt blood sugar levels, and negatively impact gut health.

2. **Refined Carbohydrates:** Items like white bread and pastries can cause blood sugar spikes and crashes, leading to mood swings and fatigue.

3. **Processed Foods:** Often high in unhealthy fats, sodium, and artificial additives, processed foods can negatively impact brain function and mood.

4. **Excessive Caffeine:** While moderate caffeine may be beneficial, excessive consumption can lead to anxiety, insomnia, and other mental health issues.

5. **Alcohol:** As a depressant, alcohol can disrupt sleep, worsen mood, and contribute to mental health conditions.

Additional Tips for Promoting Mental Health Through Food

Alongside a healthy diet, consider these additional tips for promoting mental health through food:

1. **Practice Mindful Eating:** Pay attention to hunger and fullness cues, and savor each bite by eating slowly. It is important to remember, "Eat what you drink and drink what you eat."

2. **Cook More Meals at Home:** Preparing meals at home allows you to control ingredients and portion sizes.

3. **Eat with Others:** Sharing meals with friends and family fosters social connections and reduces stress.

4. **Don't Be Afraid to Experiment:** Explore new recipes and discover healthy foods that you enjoy.

Conclusion

For optimal physical and mental well-being, prioritize fresh fruits, salads, and hydration with 8 to 10 glasses of water daily. Embrace a wise approach to nutrition by choosing foods in their natural state while avoiding fried, fast, and processed foods. Remember, if you are struggling with a mental health condition, seeking professional help is essential. A doctor or therapist can provide personalized guidance and support. There is a wise saying, "Nutrition is the queen, exercise is the king. Bring them together, and you will get the kingdom (of health).

***

The Dark Side of the Clock: Regulating Mental Health While Working Night Shifts

Dr. (Col.) Rajinder Singh

Former Senior Advisor, Psychiatry, Armed Forces

November 1, 2023

In our 24/7 working world, many industries rely on night shifts to keep operations running smoothly. While these shifts are essential for the economy and society, they can significantly affect workers' mental health. Disruption of the body's natural circadian rhythms, isolation from the regular day-to-day world, and lack of sleep can create a perfect storm of challenges for those working nights. This blog explores the impact of night shifts on mental health and provides strategies to help those facing these unique challenges.

The Night Shift Struggle

1. **Disrupted Circadian Rhythms:** Our bodies are wired to be active during the day and rest at night. Night shifts disrupt this natural order, making it difficult to establish a consistent sleep schedule. This disruption can lead to a host of problems, including sleep disorders, fatigue, and mood swings, as the body struggles to adapt to a new sleep-wake cycle.

2. **Isolation and Loneliness:** Night shift workers often find themselves isolated from the rest of the world. While most people sleep, these employees are working, which can lead to feelings of loneliness. Missing out on social activities and events can contribute to increased feelings of depression and anxiety.

3. **Sleep Deprivation:** Sleep is essential for maintaining good mental health. Night shift workers often struggle to get adequate rest during the day, as their sleep can be disrupted by noise, light, and other environmental factors. Chronic sleep deprivation can lead to irritability, impaired cognitive function, and a heightened risk of mood disorders.

4. **Increased Risk of Mental Health Issues:** Studies show that night shift workers face a greater risk of mental health issues, such as depression and anxiety. The combination of disrupted sleep patterns, isolation, and chronic fatigue can exacerbate pre-existing conditions and challenge individuals' emotional well-being.

5. **Melatonin Disruption:** Night shifts can disrupt melatonin production, a hormone that regulates the sleep-wake cycle. Typically released during the night, artificial light exposure during shifts can suppress melatonin, making it difficult for workers to fall asleep during the day.

6. **Higher Risk of Diseases:** Night shifts can disrupt the production of growth hormones, elevate the risks of diabetes and hypertension, and are associated with an increased risk of certain cancers. This underscores the need for vigilant health management among night shift workers.

Coping Strategies for Night Shift Workers

While working night shifts can be challenging, several strategies can help alleviate their impact on mental health:

1. **Prioritize Sleep:** Create a sleep-conducive environment at home. Invest in blackout curtains, earplugs, and a comfortable mattress to improve the quality of your daytime sleep.

2. **Maintain a Consistent Schedule:** Stick to a consistent sleep-wake schedule, even on your days off. This can help regulate your circadian rhythms and ease the transition between day and night shifts.

3. **Practice Self-Care:** Engage in self-care activities like meditation, exercise, and hobbies. These can reduce stress and enhance your overall well-being.

4. **Seek Professional Help:** If you're struggling with your mental health, don't hesitate to seek professional assistance. A therapist or counselor can provide tailored support and coping strategies.

5. **Consider Your Diet:** Pay attention to your nutrition. Eating a balanced diet and avoiding heavy, rich foods before bedtime can improve your sleep quality.

Conclusion

Working night shifts can be mentally and emotionally taxing, but it's possible to mitigate the impact on your mental health with the right strategies and support. By prioritizing sleep, staying connected, and practicing self-care, night shift workers can work toward maintaining their mental well-being and leading fulfilling lives despite the challenges of their schedules. Remember, your mental health is just as important as your physical health, and seeking help when needed is a sign of strength, not weakness.

***

Watch Out for These Five Mental Health Symptoms in Your Family

Dr. (Col.) Rajinder Singh

Former Senior Advisor, Psychiatry, Armed Forces

Mental health is vital for overall well-being and can affect anyone, including your family members. Recognizing symptoms and addressing them early is crucial. In this blog, we'll discuss five common mental health symptoms to watch for in your loved ones, along with practical ways to help.

1. Persistent and Extreme Mood Changes

Symptom: Frequent and intense mood swings, such as overwhelming sadness or euphoria, that disrupt daily life.

Tackle It: Encourage open communication and consider professional help through therapy or medication.

2. Social Withdrawal and Isolation

Symptom: Avoidance of social interactions and increasing isolation from friends and family.

Tackle It: Be supportive without applying pressure, and suggest low-key social activities or seek professional guidance.

3. Changes in Sleep Patterns

Symptom: Significant disruptions in sleep patterns, such as insomnia or excessive sleepiness.

Tackle It: Establish a consistent sleep routine and encourage relaxation techniques to improve sleep quality.

4. Unexplained Physical Symptoms

Symptom: Physical complaints with no apparent medical cause, such as headaches or stomach aches.

Tackle It: Consult a healthcare professional and promote a healthy lifestyle through exercise and a balanced diet.

5. Decline in Daily Functioning

Symptom: Noticeable difficulty in carrying out daily tasks and responsibilities, or a loss of interest in activities once enjoyed.

Tackle It: Offer practical support, encourage seeking a professional mental health assessment, and promote self-care practices for recovery.

Conclusion

Mental health affects us all, and recognizing these five common symptoms in your family members is the first step toward providing the support they need. Encourage open communication, offer understanding, and gently suggest seeking professional help when necessary. By addressing these symptoms and promoting well-being through healthy routines and self-care, you can help your loved ones on their journey toward mental health recovery. Remember, your support can make a significant difference in their lives, enabling them to lead happier and more fulfilling lives ahead.

***

Mental Health and COVID-19

Dr. (Col.) Rajinder Singh

Former Senior Advisor, Psychiatry, Armed Forces

October 4, 2020

Mental health encompasses psychological, physical, and social well-being. A mentally healthy individual can cope with everyday challenges, engage in social activities, and lead a fulfilling life. Since the dawn of civilization, humanity has sought happiness—not only for ourselves but for all living creatures. Animals, birds, and aquatic beings have simple desires for food and shelter, thriving in their natural habitats. However, humans have lost touch with nature and have often destroyed the environments of other species.

Despite scientific discoveries and technological advancements making our lives more comfortable, this progress hasn't led to a proportional increase in happiness. We find ourselves in misery because we cling to a hedonistic viewpoint that equates well-being solely with the pursuit of pleasure and the avoidance of suffering.

For centuries, homo-sapiens have been devastating the environment, leading to the collapse of biodiversity, the degradation of ecosystems, increased carbon dioxide levels, and global warming. Deforestation has contributed to the emergence of viruses from animals to humans and the extinction of species. Scientists estimate that over 150 to 200 species of plants, insects, birds, and mammals become extinct every 24 hours. Approximately 200 million animals are slaughtered worldwide, and when including farmed fish and other livestock, that number rises to three billion animals killed daily for food. Alarmingly, around 300 wild sea animals are killed each year to feed a single American.

The Holy Hymn from the Sri Guru Granth Sahib Ji reminds us: *'Awar Jon Teri Panhari / Is Dharti Mahe Teri Sikdari'* (Sri Guru Granth Sahib, 373), meaning that all other living creatures are your servants, and in this world, you are the ruler. As the rulers of the earth, we bear responsibility for these startling figures.

In contrast, Bhutan, a small country with a population of 700,000, has made extraordinary achievements in environmental conservation. It is the only country in the world that is carbon-negative, removing more carbon than it produces due to 60% of its land being forested. Killing any living creature is illegal, and tobacco is banned. Bhutan emphasizes Gross National Happiness (GNH) over Gross Domestic Product (GDP), with a constitutional obligation for every citizen to protect the environment. Consequently, Bhutan stands as one of the happiest and greenest countries globally.

The COVID-19 pandemic has taken a heavy toll on human life, with many individuals exhibiting signs of stress, anxiety, and depression. Rates of suicide and relapse among those with mental illnesses have risen significantly. Factors contributing to this mental health crisis include confinement due to lockdowns, loneliness, financial difficulties, unemployment, lack of sunlight exposure, and fear of contracting the virus. Domestic violence has also surged, prompting United Nations Secretary-General António Guterres to call for protections for women facing violence during this crisis.

Interestingly, research during the lockdown period—more than 300 studies reported in *Science Magazine*—showed a beneficial impact on wildlife. Species such as mammals, reptiles, birds, and fish exhibited less fear and stress. With decreased human movement and activity worldwide, wildlife breathed easier, and pollution levels declined.

In their book *Our Only Home*, the Dalai Lama and German environmentalist Franz Alt discuss climate change and advocate for holistic education that emphasizes the interrelatedness of life through scientifically informed learning. They observe, "The Earth is our home, and it is on fire. It is common sense to take necessary steps to extinguish the flames." However, we have failed to act, leading nature to hit the 'anthropause' button.

Let us heed the messages sent by the COVID-19 pandemic and the example of Bhutan:

1. The 'Ashraf-ul-makhluqat' or the human being, the crown creation of nature, must become more humane toward animals and wildlife. This may require modifications to our lifestyle and a willingness to step out of our comfort zones.

2. All nations must follow Bhutan's noble example and make coordinated efforts to reduce greenhouse gas emissions. Countries should prioritize the choice between human development and environmental degradation.

3. Education should embrace a holistic approach that combines scientific learning with human values. These measures are paramount to preventing future tsunamis, hurricanes, and pandemics on our planet.

4. Lastly, Albert Schweitzer, a Nobel Peace Prize winner and known for his philosophy of "reverence for life", wrote, "As long as we do not show kindness to living creatures, we cannot ask for World Peace."